SPORTING LODGES

Sanctuaries, Havens and Retreats

SPORTING LODGES

Sanctuaries, Havens and Retreats

J C Jeremy Hobson and David S D Jones

Quiller

Copyright © 2013 J C Jeremy Hobson & David S D Jones

First published in the UK in 2013
by Quiller, an imprint of Quiller Publishing Ltd

British Library Cataloguing-in-Publication Data
A catalogue record for this book
is available from the British Library

ISBN 978 1 84689 168 7

Book and jacket design by Sharyn Troughton
Printed in China

Quiller

An imprint of Quiller Publishing Ltd

Wykey House, Wykey, Shrewsbury, SY4 1JA
Tel: 01939 261616 Fax: 01939 261606
E-mail: info@quillerbooks.com
Website: www.countrybooksdirect.com

CONTENTS

ACKNOWLEDGEMENTS

❧

A BOOK OF THIS NATURE would be impossible without historical research; the sources of which are covered both in the text and in the 'Bibliography'. Additional, up-to-date and personal assistance is, however, imperative, and for that we have to thank all of the following:

Jack Gratton; Robert Bowman; Erbil Arkin; John Walker; George Rolls; Robin Chute; Sue Knight; Rhoderick Macleod; Iain Thornber; Tony Morrison; Geoff Burch; Oliver Pope at the Wrackleford Estate, Dorset; the Countess of Carnarvon and Candice Bauval at Highclere Castle, Berkshire; Mike Davies at Damerham Fisheries; James Cooper, director at Stansted Park, Hampshire; Marion Martineau, owner of Moses Hill Farm, Surrey and Mike Barnes, editor of *The Scottish Sporting Gazette* – for his extremely useful lodge 'leads'. Richard Hughes helped immensely in providing information relating to the Palethorpe family's shooting activities on Anglesey. Similarly, in Scotland, the assistance of Cree MacKenzie of Scaliscro Lodge, Isle of Lewis; Simon Scott and Debbie Millar at Grimersta Lodge, Isle of Lewis and Ian Scarr-Hall and Judi Dolton at Amhuinnsuidhe Castle on the Isle of Harris, proved invaluable.

Evocative memories and recollections of life in the lodge came from the late Elizabeth Macinnes of Balallan in the Hebrides, and Helen Spellman – who was kind enough to put pen to paper and write of her life at Fermoyle Lodge, Co. Galway. Some of their material we have been able to reproduce verbatim and it gives a real first-hand glimpse of what life was really like in the sporting lodges.

Thanks must also go to Quiller Publishing for allowing us to quote from Peter Holt's *The Keen Foxhunter's Miscellany* and also Jonathan Ruffer's book, *The Big Shots*. Jeremy Clarke and the Felbridge and District History Group were gracious enough to permit the use of their archive photos – and the 'communications team' at English Heritage most certainly lived up to their name and 'communicated' unbelievably promptly when we sought out information and photographs appertaining to the Sir Thomas Tresham's triangular lodge at Rushton, Northamptonshire: their particular contribution to this book is very much appreciated. Andrew and Jacquie Pern at The Star Inn, Harome, North Yorkshire were also incredibly forthcoming in allowing us to quote from Andrew's book, *Black Pudding & Fois Gras*, and in providing the wonderfully atmospheric photograph of a shooting lunch in progress.

In *The Field* magazine of a few years ago, Bobby McAlpine was named as one of the '100 Best Shots' of all time. He also runs the Llanarmon shoot in North Wales, which is listed as one of the best fifty sporting estates in Britain and we are extremely grateful to him for his willingness to help and allow access to photos and information. Equally as kind were the Countess Sondes and Elizabeth Roberts at Lees Court, Kent; John Giffard, CBE, QPM, DL, at Chillington Hall, Staffordshire; Martyn Greswolde; Paul Sedgewick and Andrew Phillips of the Yattendon estate, Berkshire. Rupert Acton at Acton Scott estate, Church Stretton, Shropshire, also readily gave of his time – and photographs – of his charming shooting lodge. Graham Downing, writer and photographer, was most generous in allowing us the use of his superb photos appertaining to Charles Cotton's fishing house on the River Dove.

As far as help and the use of photographs are concerned, we further wish to thank the following: Mike Morant, railway photographer and archivist of note – for information and permission to use illustrative material appertaining to *The Flying Scotsman*; Ed Waddington at Teffont Magna, Wiltshire; Dean and Jo Harris at the Squirrel's Hall shoot; Jeremy Finnis, owner of Dell, Inverness-shire; Anthea Busk at Houghton Lodge, Stockbridge, Hampshire; Dick Bronks at the East Lodge Fishery, Twyford, Hampshire; Howard Taylor, owner of Upstream Dry-Fly (www.upstreamdryfly.com); Alick Barnes at Loyton Lodge; Helen Costello, general manager of Hotel Endsleigh, Dartmoor; Kevin Bramhill at The Cleeve, Porlock, Somerset; Alexandra Papadakis, owner of the Monkey Island Hotel, Bray, and Katrina Fossey, meetings and events co-ordinator at Monkey Island – to whom none of our requests seemed too much trouble.

Other photos are included by courtesy of Bobby McAlpine; Geremy Thomas; Mandy Shepherd; PDG Helicopters Ltd; the families Thornton, Holmes and Dempster; K R Mackay; C G Hallam; James Scott-Harden; M B Macdonald; Rupert Stephenson; Tony Moss; Charlie Caminada; Plankbridge Hutmakers and the Pairc Historical Society.

Our appreciation extends also to all those people with whom we've had casual conversations regarding sourcing suitable material and who have put us on the right track – sadly, some did so without our even having chance to learn their name…their help and advice is, though, much appreciated.

Final thanks must go to 'Google' – that modern fount of all knowledge, through which an amazing amount of information appertaining to sporting lodges can be discovered!

Whilst every reasonable effort has been made to contact all copyright owners in whatever context, if we have omitted anyone or made errors, we can only apologise and request that those affected contact the publishers in order that amends may be made in any subsequent printing of this publication.

J C Jeremy Hobson
David S D Jones
Summer 2013

Authors' note: It is essential that the reader acknowledges the fact that we have, wherever possible, attempted to avoid using inclusive pronouns (e.g. 'his or her' and 'he and she') in the text: sometimes though, for pure convenience, it has been necessary and convenient to use 'he' as a neutral pronoun and we would ask that absolutely no sexist inference is taken from this.

Contemporary photographs by Jeremy Hobson unless otherwise stated and credited.

Black and white photographs and other archive materials are the copyright/property of The David S D Jones Collection unless otherwise stated and credited.

The jacket photographs are credited as follows: (*front top*) Rupert Acton; (*front bottom and back top*) Graham Downing; (*bottom left*) Amhuinnsuidhe Castle Estate; (*centre right*) The David S D Jones Collection; (*bottom right*) Howard Taylor www.upstreamdryfly.com

INTRODUCTION

❧

'WHERE WE MEET'

IT WOULDN'T BE TOO WRONG TO ASSUME THAT, some 15,000 years ago, when our ancestors were taking shelter in caves, foraging for naturally-occurring plants and hunting for animals as food and providers of skins, they would have met at a central point before setting out. Man is not naturally a solitary beast anyway and, when being unsure as to what dangers might be just around the corner, it made very good sense to hunt in groups; not only for safety's sake, but also for efficiency and maximum productivity. In all likelihood, the meeting point would have been in front of the 'chief's' temporary abode or, as time progressed and life became less nomadic, at the most central part of a settlement.

In that, things are still similar these days! Where, for instance, might a pack of hounds traditionally meet if not in front of the local landowner's mansion or on the village green …or outside a public house, itself normally situated in a central part of hamlet or town?

Many pubs and country hotels are filled during the shooting season by teams of roving syndicates who shoot at one estate one day and drive on to another the next.

If the location is right for shooting purposes, then there's a pretty good chance that, in the summer months, the surrounding countryside can also offer some superb fishing in the rivers which flow along the bottom of the valleys over which pheasant and partridge are driven at other times. The Guns and fishermen may well be met there by shoot captain or ghillie and it is almost certain that there'll be a rod or gun room in which participants can congregate at both the beginning and end of the day.

Fishing lodges are, arguably, set in the best locations – who cannot fail to be charmed by a thatched edifice on the banks of a southern chalk stream… or by a hut in Scotland from where, as was recently described, one can gaze at 'the impeccably kept lawn that sweeps gently down to the most inviting sweep of water…which is…enough to make even the mildest salmon aficionado's mouth water'?

If they can be accommodated, sporting guests may possibly be invited to stay at the host's house – at the very least, they will probably meet there and, either in the dining room or tucked away in a lunch hut, eat a midday meal amongst like-minded enthusiasts. The same room will serve as a place to finish the day with tea and cake…and to give Guns opportunity to meet the keeper and thank him for a great day's sport.

Hardier sporting souls, those who think nothing of rising before dawn in order to get out on the mud flats for wildfowling and duck-flighting, wander the cold winter river-banks for grayling, or who follow the fell hounds across the wildest of terrain, will most likely forgo such luxuries and meet their sporting colleagues either in a pre-arranged car-park, at a signed crossroads, or well-known topographical point.

FROM AUSTERITY TO OPULENCE

On the subject of fell-hunting, as Jill Mason mentions in her wonderfully researched book *Away; My Lads, Away*, '…it was commonplace for a pack to hunt an area for a week staying on farms where a bed and meals were always provided for the huntsman and a warm dry barn for his hounds along with a boiling pot to cook their porridge.'

In Scotland, the first shooting lodges were originally referred to as 'quarters' and were quite primitive affairs offering basic accommodation for the sporting visitors who made the long and arduous journey north to the Highlands by sea and horse-drawn conveyance during the first part of the 1800s. Invariably ex-servicemen, who were used to living in Spartan conditions on the battlefield, at sea or in the Colonies, they quite happily decamped for the summer and early autumn in a simple stone-walled and thatched building and were looked after by a manservant who usually acted as valet, cook and ghillie. By the latter part of the century, however and, following Queen Victoria's acquisition of the Balmoral estate for sporting purposes, deer stalking, grouse shooting and salmon fishing had started to become a fashionable pastime amongst the rich and the famous – in particular newly rich businessmen who had made money in brewing, in manufacturing or in the City of London. Unlike their predecessors, these sportsmen, who often rented Highland estates for status reasons as much as for sport, expected good quality accommodation and set about constructing rather more comfortable lodges to house both them and their guests.

BUILT TO LAST

Like many things, the word 'lodge' came to Britain with the Normans, and was derived from a Frankish (According to *Collins*: 'the ancient West Germanic language of the Franks, especially the dialect that contributed to the vocabulary of modern French') word for shelter – and therefore suggests either a temporary building or one in which people stayed for only a short length of time. Whilst the occupants might, in the heyday of such places, indeed only have lived there on a seasonal basis, there was nothing temporary about the construction of many sporting lodges and, in certain parts of the country, there still exist places of Victorian and Edwardian design that will last for many years to come. In Scotland (and some parts of the West Country), a great many of these places are in fine fettle and are still a short-term home to groups of enthusiastic men and women who travel annually in order to indulge in their chosen pastime. Elsewhere in Britain, though, it is a sad fact that not many are nowadays used for their original purpose and are instead, private houses, holiday lets, youth hostels, training schools and conference centres. Fortunately, a few important ones are also in the capable and caring hands of English Heritage, the National Trust and the National Trust for Scotland.

ALL THINGS TO ALL MEN

Many of the original 'lodges' were built and then maintained for all manner of sporting purposes: seasonally, they might accommodate fishermen, riders to hounds, stalkers and game shooters and it is precisely for this reason that we have, throughout this book, made reference to much more than just shooting lodges – most notably in the section headed *Location; Location, Location* where the subject of hunting 'boxes' and fishing huts also get good mention. We make no apologies for this as it is all part of the fascinating history – and modern-day use – of how and why things are as they are today.

Finally, whilst on the subject of hunting 'boxes', it is as well to note that, in many places of Britain - but for some reason, mainly in the wilder moorland areas – what might be termed shooting lodges elsewhere are, in these regions, more usually known as shooting 'boxes'…as to the term 'bothy' sometimes being used to describe certain sequestered buildings…read on!!!

HOW THE LODGE CAME ABOUT

❧

SEEN BY MANY AS A VICTORIAN INSTITUTION, where wealthy sportsmen could stay in the field in 'home from home' comfort whilst shooting, fishing or hunting, the sporting lodge is in fact deeply rooted in history. The very first were erected in Royal forests and chases during Norman and Medieval times in order to provide accommodation for the monarch and favoured noblemen when hunting deer, wild boar and other quarry species. Some of these lodges eventually became country seats for members of the aristocracy whilst still serving as shooting lodges during the sporting season.

As a prime example of this, Rushmore Lodge, on the Wiltshire-Dorset border, was for centuries, a royal hunting residence where the keeper of the Cranborne Chase lived, and where courts were held to implement laws governing the preservation of deer on the chase. Rushmore was later to become the property of the Pitt family and re-built as a Georgian country house in 1760 by George Pitt (later 1st Lord Rivers), a member of parliament for Dorset. Forever a keen sportsman, Rivers kept a pack of buckhounds at the property and hawked woodcock and other game birds on the surrounding downs. Both he and his immediate successors used Rushmore as a hunting box, and carried out the duties of the feudal Lord of the Chase until Cranborne chase was disenfranchised in 1828.

Generally though, other than the various royal lodges that were scattered around the country and those erected for eminent members of the nobility and the clergy who possessed royal sporting rights, sporting lodges were few and far between until the early years of the nineteenth century. Indeed, it was not until the Game Act of 1831 removed the restrictions imposed upon game shooting by Henry VIII (but which also established close seasons for legally defined species of game), that lodge building really got off the ground.

Namesake George Pitt, the 4th Lord Rivers, eventually converted Rushmore into his shooting lodge and summer residence, spending the remainder of each year at Mistley Hall in Essex (his principal seat) and at subsidiary houses in London and Torquay. An enthusiastic shot, he transferred Robert Grass, his Mistley head keeper, to Rushmore in 1840 in order to establish a pheasant shoot on the property and develop the existing partridge shooting. Rushmore continued to serve as a shooting lodge until 1880 when it became the country home of the Pitt-Rivers family. In 1939, the lodge began a new lease of life as a preparatory school, housing Sandroyd School, the current occupiers. (Incidentally, the Pitt-Rivers museum in Oxford is well worth a visit!)

NINETEENTH CENTURY SHOOTING LODGES

The first purpose-built shooting lodges in England and Wales were constructed during the early years of the nineteenth century by noblemen and other wealthy individuals in order that they could spend part of the sporting season living on either a remote part of their estate; a subsidiary estate, or distant grouse moor, and shoot or fish on the surrounding land. These lodges were often built by a local master builder, although it was not unknown for a fashionable architect to be engaged.

Some Irish landowners built shooting lodges either for the same reason or for the purpose of letting to tenants along with associated sporting rights. Invariably much smaller and far less luxurious than those found in Scotland, these lodges nevertheless found a ready market amongst the more impecunious sportsmen who were happy to spend long days out on the moor and river in wind and rain, walking-up grouse over dogs or trying their luck with salmon and sea trout on fast flowing rivers.

Some far more impressive lodges were built around this time in the North of England, the Peak district and North Wales – all with grouse shooting in mind. It is, though, in Scotland that the shooting lodge has (at least since the Victorian period), been considered part and parcel of the traditional sporting estate. Often designed to accommodate a sporting tenant and his party in country house comfort – and, in times past, a large retinue of servants – a lodge of this description could vary in size and layout between a specially constructed Scottish 'baronial' style castle or mansion, to an old established stately home, a comfortable farmhouse, or a even a refurbished and extended gamekeeper's cottage.

Wet, yet undaunted!

Not every Scottish lodge had the benefit of comfort. Particularly Spartan was the shooting lodge at Park on the Isle of Lewis in 1850: the Reverend George Hely-Hutchinson described it thus in his book, *Twenty Years Reminiscences of the Lews*, published in 1871:

A view of Aline that the Rev George Hely-Hutchinson would have undoubtedly recognised

THE GREAT DRAWBACK OF THE PARK… was, when it was part of the Aline shooting, that between the house of Aline and it lay Loch Seaforth – a beautiful picturesque object in fine weather, but in bad – which it sometimes can be in those latitudes – not the pleasantest place in the world…Moreover, there was in the whole of this Park but one small bothy, in which the sportsmen, ghillies, and stalkers could put up – and what a den it was! I shall never forget the first day we got there – wet, of course. I had shot over, Robert Morritt had stalked. The roof let in the rain, the floor was earth; more smoke came into the room than went up the chimney. But we were tired and hungry, and turned soon into those holes in the wall called 'Scottice,' bed-places. In the morning – it had rained all the night – the floor was an epitome of the Lews – land dotted with lakes; and, I remember well, we had to get turf creels or bits of old planks to lay down like hearth-rugs by our beds, to step on as we rose. But what will not determined stalkers go through?

The origin of the Scottish lodge

Of all, the Scottish shooting lodges are most deeply rooted in history, and, as we have seen, the first were likely to have been extremely primitive affairs built by clan chiefs and other major landowners so as to provide basic overnight shelter when hunting deer. George Malcolm writing in his 1910 publication, *Grouse and Grouse Moors* commented that:

THE GREAT HIGHLAND CHIEFS, when they sallied out to shoot over distant parts of their estates, were content to abide in dwellings which the autocratic sporting tenant of our day would account a social impossibility. They thought it no hardship, but an agreeable variation of their normal domesticities, to sleep in a wattled hut in the high corrie or open moor, and live on the produce, from day to day, of the gun.

The travel writer, John Leyden, describes one such similar place that he came across while compiling his *Journal of a Tour in the Highlands and Western Island of Scotland*, published in 1800:

> MACDONELL OF GLENGARRY has constructed, on the side of Loch Nevis a little above Scothouse, a wicker house in the ancient manner, to serve as a hunting-box. The form of the house and the position of the rafters seem to be exactly imitated, and there is no ceiling but the roof. Instead, however, of forming the exterior walls with turf and sods, they have injudiciously covered it with slates – an excellent idea for a virtuoso and antiquary.

Hardship no longer being seen as a necessary part of what is now known amongst today's macho youngsters by the term 'manning-up', shooting lodge conditions began to improve during the first three decades of the nineteenth century. The descendents of the aforementioned chieftains and lairds started to build more substantial lodges on their property with a view to letting shooting and fishing on a commercial basis – and to a better class of tenant who was prepared to pay more for superior accommodation. As an example, Sir Colin MacKenzie of Kilcoy was a major Ross-shire landowner who commissioned an extremely comfortable new lodge for his 26,000 acre Loch Rosque estate at Achnasheen in the late 1830s. Advertising the property in 1842, he assured prospective sporting tenants that:

> LOCH ROSQUE LODGE is a handsome and commodious cottage, romantically situated at the foot of Loch Rosque (perhaps not surpassed in the North), containing comfortable accommodation for a party or family, completely furnished with every requisite, except silver plate and linen. There are four bedrooms on the first floor, and up two upstairs, in each of which, two beds may be made up, in all twelve beds, exclusive of a large public room, kitchen, pantry, water closet and sleeping room for maid servants, with stable, double coach house, and superior dog kennels, all slated, built within a few years; as also, a house with two rooms and a closet, besides a loft above, fitted up for a gamekeeper and servants. The lodge is close to the Parliamentary or Post Road of Achnasheen (where there is a Post Office), and within a very few hours

drive of Dingwall, by the very best of roads, to and from which the Mail Curricle, carrying passengers, passes thrice a week; and there are regular carriers to Dingwall and Inverness, by whom all supplies may be obtained, and game forwarded, whence it may be conveyed, within a few days, by steam, to London. There is a vegetable garden and pony paddock attached to the lodge, for the use of sportsmen during the shooting season.

Obviously keen to attract business, Sir Colin then went on to inform sportsmen that his shootings provided an abundance of red grouse, ptarmigan, black game and red deer, adding that the trout fishing was 'equal to any in the Highlands' and could be 'enjoyed by rod or net'. He also mentioned that Loch Rosque had been 'carefully protected from poachers and all kinds of vermin'.

The fashion for renting Scottish sporting estates continued to gather momentum throughout the 1840s (particularly after Queen Victoria and Prince Albert had acquired the Balmoral estate). As a consequence of which, it rapidly became the custom amongst the rich and the famous to spend the sporting season north of the border. However, unlike their predecessors, these sportsmen – who often took estates for status reasons as much as for sport – expected good quality accommodation with comfortable furnishings and proper dining and washing facilities; all of which led to further historical development of the lodge.

The financial aspect

Equipped with the latest in domestic furnishings and decorated with Landseer paintings, the typical Scottish castle type lodges not infrequently stretched the resources of their aristocratic builders. For instance, not content with erecting one lodge, the 7th Earl of Dunmore, owner of the Isle of Harris in the Outer Hebrides, erected two castles for the benefit of potential sporting tenants on his North Harris estate. His Gothic revival style Ardvourlie Castle stood at the head of Loch Seaforth and was built in 1863, whilst the hugely impressive Scottish baronial style Amhuinnsuidhe Castle (designed by the leading Scottish architect, David Bryce), was begun in 1865 and completed in 1868. By that time almost bankrupt, Dunmore was obliged to sell the entire estate three years later in 1871 to the London banker, Sir Edward Scott (for the sum of £155,000) in order that he might pay off his creditors and save the remainder of Harris and Dunmore Park (the latter being his Stirlingshire seat) for his successors.

Some landowners found it more profitable to sell or lease large tracts of land to wealthy Victorian businessmen who laid out sporting estates on land formerly

Alladale Lodge (*courtesy of Iain Thornber*)

used for sheep farming and constructed their own shooting lodges – often in relatively inaccessible locations. Many of these privately built shooting lodges were designed to incorporate the latest modern conveniences, affording the owner and his guests a level of comfort similar to that which could be enjoyed either at his London home or English country seat.

All 'mod-cons'

As an example of how keen the Scottish lairds were to encourage sporting business, it is appropriate to further mention Sir Colin Mackenzie of Kilcoy who, as is evidenced above, provided a primitive water closet at Loch Rosque Lodge in Ross-shire as early as the late 1830s. He was, though, not alone: Sir John Fowler, the engineer and designer of the Forth Rail Bridge, installed a water supply, a 'state of the art' sanitation system and electric lighting powered by a hydro-electric plant in his lodge at Braemore (overlooking Loch Broom in Ross-shire). Mr Joseph Platt, lessee of the 69,000 acre Park deer forest on the Isle of Lewis,

Eishken Lodge as it was not long after being built in the late 1880s (*courtesy of K R Mackay*)

not only built a substantial modern lodge at Eishken, but also laid out miles of roads and stalking tracks, and, in 1886, paid the Post Office just over £10 to open a Telegraph Office in a nearby village so as to enable him to keep in touch with the outside world on a daily basis.

Examples though the aforementioned may be, the fact remains that most of the wealthier lodge owners and tenants were equally as quick to embrace the latest technological innovations just as soon as they became available: producing their own electricity by water or acetylene, subscribing to the telephone service and acquiring primitive radio sets.

The larger shooting lodges invariably contained a dining room, two or three drawing rooms, a billiard room, a gun room, a dozen or more guest bedrooms, a bathroom (apparently an essential requirement before King Edward VII would visit as he demanded a private bathroom for his sole use!) and lavatories, as well as a kitchen and other domestic offices and extensive servants' quarters. Some even boasted a library, a ballroom and a chapel (of which more in *Outbuildings and Adjuncts* – and also in *Customs, Traditions and Curiosities*).

The golden age…and beyond

Many shooting lodges, but particularly those located in Scotland, enjoyed a golden age from the early 1880s until the declaration of war in 1914. During this period wealthy aristocrats and businessmen rented lodges and their surrounding estates or deer forests for the entire season, bringing with them family and friends, most of whom would shoot, fish or stalk, or, if of a non-sporting disposition, walk, sketch and paint.

By the Edwardian era, there were an estimated 200 deer forests and over 3,150 grouse general shootings throughout Scotland, virtually all of which had a lodge of some description – either purpose built, or by means of adapting an ancestral home, large farmhouse or hotel. The contribution which these lodges and sporting estates made to the local economy was immense; not only in terms of employment and through the purchase of goods and services from local businesses, but also through the payment of high sporting rates (often levied at between £500 and £1,000 per individual property).

The effects of The Great War

A great many shooting lodges were 'mothballed' for the duration of the First World War owing to travel restrictions imposed under the Defence of the Realm

Act, which meant that sportsmen exempt from military service or engaged upon civilian duties on the 'Home Front' could not travel north to shoot, fish or to stalk.

Several of the larger shooting lodges were used as temporary barracks, as military hospitals and as convalescent homes, while a large number of the smaller or more remote lodges were put under the charge of a local caretaker who kept the home fires burning throughout the winter months and arranged for any leaking roofs and windows to be repaired.

High taxation and death duties imposed by Lloyd George's Liberal government in the aftermath of the First World War – followed by a general decline in the sporting estate letting market – led to several shooting lodge owners either scaling down expenditure upon their properties or renting them out to hoteliers or non-sporting occupants. Some even demolished lodges, replacing them with smaller buildings which required less maintenance. Sadly, a number of lodges were also destroyed by fire during this period (was an insurance claim involved, we wonder?!).

The following years

For the next four decades or so, a significant number of shooting lodges were kept going on a shoestring basis with a skeleton staff who looked after short term sporting tenants or estate owners who could still afford to spend the summer and autumn in Scotland in pursuit of grouse, salmon or stags. By the 1960s, a renewed interest in Scottish sporting activities, both by British sportsmen and overseas clients, encouraged many estate owners (much as their forebears did) to repair or renovate run-down shooting lodges, installing additional bathrooms, fitted carpets and other modern conveniences in order to attract wealthy paying guests who preferred their home comforts to the somewhat dated accommodation that was acceptable to the more traditional sportsman.

Far more recently, a great many shooting lodges have been refurbished to a very high standard (some with original late nineteenth century fixtures and fittings to create a Victorian or Edwardian atmosphere!). Furthermore, several of the more prestigious lodges are now not only equipped with broadband internet facilities, satellite television and a mobile phone mast in order that sporting guests can keep in touch with the outside world at all times but also have a helicopter landing pad. Some lodges even produce their own 'green electricity' using a wind generator!

'New builds'

In addition to those which have been renovated, some impressive new lodges have been constructed as a replacement for older, high maintenance buildings. On the island of Lewis in the Outer Hebrides, the late Robin Davidson demolished Morsgail Lodge – a crumbling Victorian mansion – in 1985 and replaced it with a smaller, modern lodge which nowadays provides a far more comfortable and homely lodge for tenants. In Inverness-shire, the Victorian Corrour Lodge on the edge of Rannoch Moor, was destroyed by fire in 1942 and has since been replaced by a new modernistic building. This particular edifice, designed by the Boston based architect Moshe Safdie, was completed in 2003 and has subsequently been described by the Royal Fine Art Commission for Scotland as being 'one of the few examples of world class twenty-first century architecture in Scotland'. Many more (including Corrour Lodge), boast a range of en-suite bedrooms and a sauna, and offer world-class hospitality to guests.

As can be seen, although a quintessentially Victorian 'institution', the shooting lodge has nevertheless adapted to the changing times and continues to serve as the focal point of many sporting estates, providing a warm welcome for today's sportsmen and women and their families – as well as much needed employment in rural areas.

Detail of Morsgail Lodge (*from a painting the property of Sir Andrew de la Rue, Bt*)

FISHING

During the seventeenth century, fishing for pleasure resulted in the construction of some quite elaborate architect designed fishing pavilions on several English estates. No making do with rough-hewn timber planking and a thatched or corrugated tin roof for this lot of sportsmen: these buildings, which most often overlooked the waters to be fished, were often shaped in a Chinese or similar Oriental style and were given grand-sounding names of pavilions or temples.

On an island in the River Thames, near the village of Bray in Berkshire, are situated possibly two of the most unusual buildings of this nature. Nowadays standing in the grounds of the Monkey Island Hotel, the fishing lodge and fishing

Charles Spencer had the fishing pavilion on Monkey Island constructed of wood made to look like stone…

…and an ornate ceiling painted by the artist Andieu de Clermont

Under the pavilion's fanciful ceiling paintings is a simply furnished restful room…nowadays used for intimate meals

temple were, in fact, the first buildings on the site and were erected in 1723 under the instructions of Charles Spencer, 3rd Duke of Marlborough. Spencer was a very enthusiastic angler – and also very imaginative with his designs for both buildings are nothing at all like the average fishing lodge! There is, for example, the somewhat quirky fact that the Duke had the Pavilion built out of wood blocks cut to look like stone – surely it would have been easier to have built with stone blocks in the first place? Originally, the Temple building was open on the ground floor: nowadays it is enclosed and has the addition of doors and windows. On the ceiling of the room overhead (now a part of the hotel) are some fine examples of Wedgwood-style high-relief plasterwork.

It is though, the ceiling of the Pavilion that defies belief for there, painted some time prior to 1738, by French artist Andieu de Clermont, can be observed the strangest and most wonderful scenes depicting monkeys engaged in all manner of country-related humanistic activities.

Then and now

Today, it is not uncommon for English or Welsh anglers with their own small stretch of water to purchase a weekend cottage, flat or caravan in the vicinity. In the past, things were done on a far grander scale and, in Hampshire, for example, Lord Northbrook and Sir Edward Grey, both members of the six strong trout fishing syndicate who rented the Avington section of the river Itchen near Winchester during the late nineteenth century, obtained convenient local lodges by, in one case, building one and, in the other, adapting a bungalow already in existence near the hallowed river bank! The ever increasing interest in fishing for sporting purposes in the late-eighteenth and the nineteenth centuries led to the construction of residential fishing lodges adjacent to a number of well known English rivers in order to provide accommodation for itinerant anglers who leased stretches of water or fished on a 'grace and favour' basis with permission of the riparian owner.

Houghton Lodge at Stockbridge in Hampshire, a *cottage ornée* style house on the banks of the river Test, built sometime prior to 1799 at the instruction of Maurice Bernard, a Lincoln's Inn barrister, is known to have been originally commissioned as a fishing lodge for summer vacations. The original structure was timber-framed, perfectly symmetrical and the roof was thatched. Outbuildings included stabling for fourteen horses and four carriages (the stable block has since been incorporated into the main house) and a brew-house complete with well and oven. Still privately owned, the present occupants

The fishing lodge at Houghton, Hampshire; a *cottage ornée* style house situated
on the banks of the famous River Test

continue to fish and let out fishing on their stretch of the river – as well as open
their quite glorious gardens to public view.

Over the border

Dedicated residential fishing lodges were built at various locations in Scotland
– due in no small part to the expanding rail and steamer networks, which
enabled angling enthusiasts to access a wide range of hitherto remote rivers.
These lodges ranged from primitive stone-walled and thatched bothies or tiny
wooden huts to grandiose prefabricated buildings manufactured in kit form in
the nearest towns and transported by train or boat to the most suitable pier or
railhead before then being taken to site by horse and cart for assembly!

The first lodge at Grimersta on the Isle of Lewis (one of the earliest purpose-
built Scottish fishing lodges), constructed circa 1856 to provide accommodation
for wealthy anglers visiting the river, was certainly not designed with comfort

in mind. John Mackay, for many years head keeper at Grimersta, described the lodge in his unpublished memoirs as it was in 1866:

> THE PLACE was quite unprotected, without dyke, fence, or wall of any kind. The house, which was built on the site of the present lodge, consisted of a low, narrow, building, the walls being only about six feet high. There were five small apartments which served as bedrooms for anglers. One apartment, twelve feet square, served as dining and sitting room combined. At the other end was a kitchen, and maid's room. As there was no water laid on, the whole supply had to be carried in, in buckets. The ghillie's bothy was at the north end of the lodge, a single apartment building, with a straw roof.

In 1871, the lessees replaced the lodge with a more modern prefabricated lodge clad in local stone, which included six bedrooms, an inside toilet and Victorian style iron stair furnishings. In contrast, the Norwegian style Finsbay Lodge on the Isle of Harris, built in 1903 by a wealthy angling syndicate, known as The Hebridean Sporting Association, was the last word in luxury. Constructed at the cost of £2,500 (about £150,000 in today's prices) from a pre-made kit of timber and corrugated iron shipped in from the mainland, the lodge contained

Grimersta Lodge as it is today (*courtesy of the Grimersta Estate*)

over twenty guest bedrooms; three bathrooms with hot and cold water supplies and flush toilets; a smoking room, a dining room, a drawing room, two sitting rooms and generous servants' quarters. The lodge was so large, in fact, that a manager was engaged to run it along the lines of a hotel.

Later Scottish purpose-built fishing lodges were far less pretentious than Finsbay. Indeed, after the First World War, many sportsmen who bought or leased river beats from major landowners acquired ex-army huts for accommodation purposes, siting them in convenient positions by river or loch and installing a resident ghillie-general factotum in a small annexe. More recently, small fishery owners have utilised local cottages, redundant croft houses, modern bungalows or caravans as seasonal fishing lodges.

HUNTING

A quick visit to any internet search engine reveals the fact that, if he'd been to all the places supposed, King John would have had no time at all for ruling the country! There are, it would seem, many 'King John's Hunting Lodges' dotted up and down the country: just three of which are located at Laycock in Wiltshire (which is now a very attractive eating place and tea-rooms), Axbridge, Somerset, (a museum) and the third, a Grade II listed building in Wraysbury, Berkshire which is a private house. Whether or not this sporting king did actually visit all these places in order to avail himself of what was on offer in the nearby forests is open to speculation, but the fact remains that it was about this time that the first hunting lodges of any description were built.

Introduced by the Normans after 1066, and the prerogative of kings and noblemen, hunting resulted in the creation of 'Royal Forests' and, within them, lodges to which participants could travel, stay and kennel their hounds. The largest and most famous of these vast tracts of hunting land was the New Forest, which, despite its name, is not new at all and even now after all these years and urbanisation, still covers some 145 square miles.

The early days of hunting – the prerogative of kings and noblemen

Poaching penalties

The penalties for any of the local commoners who dared to take deer was quite severe, if not to say draconian, and the Norman aristocracy guarded their hunting forests so intensely that anyone found poaching lost either a hand or an eye for a first offence and his life for a second. It was also a punishable offence to own a dog that stood too long in the leg and might therefore be capable of chasing and pulling down a deer.

Things were just as serious when Henry VII came to the throne: one of his first parliament acts in 1485, made poaching an offence punishable by death if the poachers did so at night or deliberately tried to disguise themselves. If, though, the felony had taken place during daylight hours, or without a disguise, only a fine or imprisonment would ensue!

A Godly sport!

Weardale near Durham, although today relatively sparsely wooded, did, like Rockingham Forest (see *Deer Coursing Grandstands* later in this chapter) and several others; have 'Royal Forest' status conferred upon it – in fact, it was, at one time, second only to the New Forest in size. Various Prince Bishops of Durham hunted over Weardale in the High Middle Ages and pursued both deer and wolves with packs of hounds which were of the deerhound type – and therefore followed their quarry by sight rather than scent. Probably the most notable of the Prince Bishops was Hugh de Puiset (1125–1195), sometimes referred to as Hugh Pudsey, who had a hunting lodge built at what is now Bishop Auckland (the area around which was then known generally as 'Aucklandshire').

From written records prepared by monks at the time, it seems that peasants under the Bishop's jurisdiction were required to build a lodge, chapel, kitchen and larder as well as provide all that might be necessary in the way of provisions. In the *Bolden Buke*, it was registered that, at West Auckland, villagers were expected to '…make the hall of the Bishop in the forest 60 feet in length and in breadth within the posts 16 feet, with a butchery and store house…And they look after the hawk eyries…Moreover…go on the roe hunt on the summons of the Bishop.' A few miles away at Stanhope, those who lived on church land (practically everybody!) had to help '…build a kitchen, and a larder and a dog kennel (for) the "Great Chases" …and lead all the Bishop's supplies from Wolsingham to the lodges'.

The Bolden Buke

Although William of Normandy took land throughout north east England and up as far as the Scottish border, they were not, for some reason, recorded in the Domesday Book and it wasn't until well over a century later that a complete audit of that area was undertaken by Bishop Hugh de Puiset (Hugh Pudsey) in 1183. One of the first places to be recorded in detail was Boldon, and what happened there became something of a blue-print for the future: for instance, throughout the ledger, the words, '…they pay taxes as at Boldon' are frequently written. The Bolden Buke is then, County Durham's equivalent of the Domesday Book.

Tudor times and beyond

Hunting and hawking were both immensely popular pastimes in the Tudor period. Again, because of the desire to carry out either sport over land where the most quarry might be found, hunting lodges were built - just a few of which are still in existence today: Newark Park in Gloucestershire was, for example, initially constructed for such a purpose in 1550…but was then converted into a family home and is now owned by the National Trust. Sadly most have disappeared - although some are being rediscovered by enthusiastic archaeologists. One such is Manor Lodge, Sheffield, which originally belonged to the Earls of Shrewsbury; another can be found at Wormingford, near Colchester, where the discovery by ferreters of some Tudor brickwork whilst rabbitting along a field hedge, has since proved to be part of a lodge built near the River Stour which runs through Essex and Suffolk.

James I used to hunt regularly in East Anglia and the parish registers for the place of Fordham record that, in 1604, '…the high and mighty Prince James, King of Great Britain, France and Ireland, Defender of the Faith…did hunt the hare with his own hounds in our fields of Fordham and did kill a hare at a place called blacklands (sic).' Apparently he so enjoyed his sport that he was a frequent guest of The Griffin inn at nearby Newmarket and, in 1608 bought the premises and some surrounding land, both of which were then used to create a very modest hunting lodge. Somewhat alarmingly, it seems that, in 1613, land subsidence resulted in the building's collapse.

Half a century or so later, far grander lodges were being built - even though they were still only ever intended to be used seasonally as temporary residences. Cliveden House at Taplow, Berkshire, was built in 1666 as a hunting lodge for

Cliveden House in Berkshire – originally built as a hunting lodge by the 2nd Duke of
Buckingham – is now a hotel owned by the National Trust

the 2nd Duke of Buckingham and was a place where he used to entertain friends
and mistresses. Converted to a magnificent hotel in 1985, one can only suppose
that some guests staying there (as with all hotels), use it for the same purpose!

The Charlton Hunt

In 1675, the Charlton Hunt was formed in West Sussex and, despite the tiny size
of the place; such was the quality of hunting and social standing of its members
that, anyone wishing to rub shoulders with royalty, nobility and gentry (and
perhaps incidentally indulge in some hunting!) had boxes in the vicinity. It was
for hunting purposes that Charles Lennox, 1st Duke of Richmond, first rented a
half-timber framed hunting lodge originally built by the Earl of Northumberland
in 1617 and then, when the opportunity to do so arose, bought the property.
The building was eventually demolished and, in its environs was created the
rather magnificent Goodwood House. In 1787, the 3rd Duke of Richmond

The old kennel buildings at Charlton, West Sussex

moved hounds from Charlton to Goodwood and had the most impressive set of kennels built (*of which more in* Outbuildings and Adjuncts).

In 1734, the Duke of Hamilton built Chatelherault as his particular hunting lodge. Situated in South Lanarkshire, Scotland, it was designed by architect William Adam (father of Robert) in the form of two pavilions linked by an ornate gateway and provided all the necessary amenities for the Duke's hunting activities. Now managed by South Lanarkshire Council, the lodge has been renovated by Historic Scotland.

The Tarpoley Club

Although it no longer has hounds, the name nowadays exists as a dining club with royal connections. Originally, though, the Tarpoley Club in Cheshire was most definitely all to do with hunting. Formed in 1762, the club pre-dated the Cheshire Hunt by a year and the place of Tarpoley was, in those early days, the venue for twice yearly meets; each of which lasted a week! One of the founders was George Wilbraham of Nantwich, later of Delamere Lodge – a place built and kept expressly for hunting purposes. Delamere Lodge was eventually renamed Delamere House and remained a family home for generations before eventually being replaced by a manor house just before World War II (Delamere Manor was, incidentally, owned and lived in for several years by Gary Barlow OBE, member of the pop group 'Take That', singer/songwriter/producer and, latterly, a judge on television's *X Factor*).

DEER COURSING GRANDSTANDS

Long before hunting as we recognise it came to the fore, it was common practice to entertain royalty and land-owning lords by organising deer driving with beaters and hounds (most likely of the 'Talbot' type brought from France by the Normans). In the Royal Forests such as Rockingham, Northamptonshire, the king and his entourage hunted from his lodge at King's Cliffe and the vast tracts of woodland were split into smaller units of perhaps twenty hectares (fifty acres) in size by means of woodbanks and fencing. In some of these would be further constructed long avenues edged off by means of paling fences, along which, were driven deer from the forest, until, at the end, they ran into an ambush of waiting bowmen. Known as 'Hayes', their locations might be guessed at by local place-names such as Fotheringhay and Sulehay.

In the Scottish Highlands, a similar system was used, except for the fact that, rather than artificial race-ways, wild deer were driven down into a ravine where they would then be taken by men and dogs lying in wait. The poet John Taylor visited Scotland in 1618 and described lords and gentlemen being situated at vantage points over a valley and beaters going out to herd the deer: '…then all the valley on each side being waylaid with a couple of hundred strong Irish grey-hounds they are let loose as occasion serves upon the herde of deer, that with dogs, gunnes, arrows durks and daggers in the space of two hours four score fat deer were slaine'.

Modern-day deerhounds

Killing and coursing in comfort

Whilst their methods were, by our standards, extremely barbaric, the degree of comfort eventually expected by some members of the land-owning classes was quite sophisticated. There are accounts of Queen Elizabeth I visiting Cowdray Park in West Sussex and there being a specially constructed turret from which she could watch, or even participate in the proceedings.

The 'sport' of shooting ambushed deer by archers with cross-bows was, over time, refined by the construction of lodges, the top part of which was open but balustraded – from which the noble onlookers would watch as park deer were driven past by dogs and either shot or brought down by gazehounds, or a combination of both. It changed further when, rather than a whole herd of deer being run past the spectators, a single stag would be pushed onto the course from the parkland enclosure. A lurcher-type dog would then persuade the beast into full stride before a couple of hounds were 'slipped' in much the way coursing greyhounds were before the 2004 Hunting Act. Half-way along the course was a post and, if the hounds had caught up with the animal before then, the competition was declared invalid. In her book *Palaces for Pigs*, Lucinda Lambton explains that the first hound to jump a ditch situated in front of the lodge and grandstand was declared the winner whilst a second, far wider ditch over which the stag could jump but the hounds could not, was a way of ensuring that the deer was able to escape.

At Lodge Park at Sherborne in Gloucestershire, there exists today a deer-coursing grandstand (now owned by the National Trust) which was built in the 1630s and has a mile and a half long coursing enclosure running in front of it. Michael Billett, in *A History of English Country Sports*, describes an even earlier building stating that it dates from the sixteenth century and was used as a hunting lodge/deer shooting stand by Queen Elizabeth I. Appropriately enough, the building, known as Great Standing, is in Ranger's Road, on the edge of Epping Forest and is nowadays, a museum.

ADAPTED BUILDINGS

Although some were purpose-built as lodges intended for seasonal use by shooting and stalking enthusiasts, fishing aficionados and followers of hounds and hawks, others were 'converted' into lodges at a later stage. And thank goodness they were because, without a need for such places, many buildings would never have been restored, and would have collapsed completely through neglect.

Farmhouses and other buildings were converted to shooting lodges. In the late 1860s, Abraham Feetham, an enterprising East Anglian gamekeeper (who is believed to be Britain's first ever shoot manager) rented The Mount at Hafod in

Cardiganshire in order to provide accommodation for sporting clients who came to shoot grouse, partridges, woodcock, hares, rabbits, snipe and wildfowl over 16,000 acres of rented land on the surrounding estate. Feetham later took a mansion house at Ponfaen in the Gwaun Valley in Pembrokeshire for similar purposes where he offered paying Guns a mixture of salmon and sea trout fishing and game bird shooting – together with an optional 'extra' of coastal seal shooting!

West Park

One example of a house that started life with one purpose and was subsequently turned into a shooting lodge can be found on the Surrey/Sussex borders. West Park (here it is of interest to note the origins of the word 'park' as it comes from the Saxon 'pearrot' or 'parwg' meaning 'a place enclosed by a paling') at first, had no connection at all to any sporting activity.

According to the Felbridge and District History Group, a building of one sort or another has been in existence on the site since the fourteenth century and had a succession of owners until being bought in 1869 by George Palmer (of Huntley and Palmer biscuits fame) – at which time, a new residence, known as West Park House was built. 'His son, Dr Alfred Palmer, used it primarily as a shooting lodge (and) extended the property in 1898…West Park House was considered to be of moderate proportions and well laid out. It contained three reception rooms, ten bedrooms and two bathrooms, with a large garage and stabling accommodation. There was a large game larder near the kitchen, as the shooting potential of the Estate was on average 800 pheasants each season, a recreation room and servants' quarters.'

West Park House in 1936…   …and as it is today (*both photos courtesy of Jeremy Clarke and the Felbridge and District History Group*)

Sadly, and again according to the Felbridge and District History Group, '…West Park House and grounds have had a chequered history. It was occupied up until 1997/8 but had been divided into bed-sit accommodation…It currently stands empty with planning consent to convert it into four houses. There is still the impression of its former grandeur, but is in need of some loving care and attention.'

Burgate Manor, Hampshire

Although not originally built for sporting purposes, Burgate Manor at Fordingbridge in Hampshire, most certainly deserves a mention in a book of this nature as it is nowadays well-known as being the headquarters of the Game and Wildlife Conservation Trust (GWCT). It was though, used briefly as a shooting and fishing lodge during the Second World War by the adventurer and explorer, Frederick A. Mitchell-Hedges (said to be the role model for the character 'Indiana Jones'). A sea angling enthusiast, Mitchell-Hedges is credited with catching a record breaking swordfish in Mexico and a 12¾ lb Wrasse at Looe in Cornwall in 1912.

Burgate Manor – nowadays home to the Game and Wildlife Conservation Trust but once used as a shooting and fishing lodge by F A Mitchell-Hedges

Acton Scott, Shropshire

Another place that started life with a different purpose entirely is the shooting lodge at Acton Scott, Church Stretton, Shropshire. It dates back to the eighteenth century and this particularly charming building (somewhat reminiscent of an American clap-board homestead) was, according to owner Rupert Acton: 'actually an old smallholding which I renamed "the Shooting Lodge" about fourteen years ago. For about ten years I used it as a shooting lodge in conjunction with the shoot I had set up at Acton Scott…and still do occasionally. Prior to this it had become derelict and was on the point of collapse. It is now one of a number of self catering holiday houses that I run.'

There is a certain amount of modesty in Rupert's words because the shooting lodge at Acton Scott has obviously had a lot of time and money spent on its restoration and is, nowadays; 'A finely restored and spacious character property…commanding uninterrupted views across open parkland towards Wenlock Edge.' Approached by a track that winds through fields and woodland, it 'retains all its original privacy and character while providing every modern

External view of the charming 'Shooting Lodge' at Acton Scott, Shropshire…

...and the interior is quite attractive too! (courtesy of Rupert Acton)

day comfort (and) includes a wealth of period features, such as beamed ceilings, oak floors and open fireplaces.'

It is of interest to note that the shooting lodge and the Acton Scott estate in general is also famous as a television location; due primarily to the fact that it achieved national fame as the setting for BBC2's hit TV series *Victorian Farm*, which was then followed by *Escape in Time*, presented by Ben Fogle.

The Star Inn at Harome

As we shall see later (in the *Cooking and Cuisine* section) hospitality, good food and shooting lodges are inextricably linked – and nowhere more so than at The Star Inn at Harome, a little village two miles south-west of Helmsley in north Yorkshire. Owned by the innovative chef Andrew Pern and his wife Jacquie, they live surrounded by prime shooting country and many of those who travel to shoot on the prestigious neighbourhood estates stay and dine at The Star – quite often in the rooms of the Lodge which, in his magnificent tome, *Black Pudding & Foie Gras* (2008), Andrew describes as being 'our "modern rustic"

A shoot lunch being enjoyed in the converted wheelhouse at Harome, North Yorkshire
(courtesy of Andrew and Jacquie Pern/The Star Inn, Harome)

accommodation …booked by the groups of shooting parties who now visit season after season, year after year…The atmosphere is of good living, of ruddy faces, of comfort and joy, and of claret-filled glasses. The converted wheelhouse with its substantial, twisted, knotted beams criss-crossing the ceiling, the feel and smell of the natural wood, the open fire giving the Lodge a feel of an alpine retreat.' All this and an incredibly wide choice of menu featuring the best produce of the area…who would not want to go there?!

LODGES WITH OTHER USES

Not all lodges were built expressly for hunting, shooting and fishing; some were constructed with a view to housing warreners responsible for keeping rabbits with which to supply the landowner fresh meat throughout the year. A few, such as at Ewden Cote on the Broomhead estate on the Derbyshire/Yorkshire borders, served a dual purpose and, although built initially to provide housing for the warrener, in the late eighteenth century, the lodge also offered shelter to the estate's shooting parties. Although the ruins of the building can still be seen, there is, according to the agents who manage the estate, nothing much in evidence of its original function.

The remains of the Warrener's Lodge near Thetford… (*courtesy of Philip Watts*)

…and how it looked in use (*courtesy of Thetford Museum*)

Some old warreners' lodges do, however, still exist in a reasonable state of repair: there's one at Thetford, Norfolk, and also at Mildenhall in Suffolk. Perhaps the most unusual and ornate however, is the three-sided warren lodge built by Sir Thomas Tresham at Rushton, Northamptonshire in the 1590s. The three-sided aspect, triangular gables, three storeys and a three-sided chimney is, apparently, all as a result of Sir Thomas's Catholic beliefs appertaining to the 'Trinity' and the Tridentine Mass.

Others that were originally constructed as warreners' lodges are now either much extended in size or in use as pubs, hotels and the like. In his fascinating book *The Archaeology of Rabbit Warrens* (Shire Books 2006), Tom Williamson mentions that Warren Cottage, built in the 1680s, in Hatfield Forest, Essex, continues to be lived in – but as a private dwelling rather than a tied cottage. In addition, The Old Lodge at Minchinhampton, Gloucestershire, being a pub in the twenty-first century, is nowadays more likely to serve beer to ferreters after a Sunday morning's sport than it is to house a warrener – which was its original purpose.

A close-up of Thomas Tresham's three-sided warrener's lodge at Rushton, Northamptonshire…

…and an aerial view showing its positioning in parkland (*both photos by courtesy of English Heritage*)

Gamekeepers' Lodges

Often known as gamekeepers' lodges rather than houses – particularly if sited in a park – the first purpose-built gamekeepers' dwellings of any description began to appear in the late eighteenth century when shooting was starting to compete against foxhunting as a popular sport. Many of these lodges were designed by Humphry Repton, John Carr and other leading architects of the period to fit in aesthetically in a landscaped country park and were either constructed in a similar style to the mansion on an estate, or in the form of a folly. In some instances, they also doubled as an entrance lodge on one of the many driveways which ran through a large estate.

As the interest in game shooting grew during the first half of the 1800s, the number of gamekeepers employed in the countryside began to increase rapidly and more and more keepers' lodges were erected. Landowners started to place lodges in strategic positions around an estate, often near areas of woodland newly planted for sporting purposes, in order that gamekeeping could be carried out in an organised manner rather than on a piecemeal basis.

Fit for purpose

Keepers' lodges were now being designed and constructed according to the status of the occupier, often in the 'model cottage' or *cottage ornée* style which was popular during the Victorian period. A beat keeper's lodge usually contained a parlour, kitchen, scullery, larder and three bedrooms, with a coal house, dog kennels, pigsty, an earth closet and a well or a pump for water outside. On some estates, lodges were also fitted with moveable partition walls on the ground floor which was able to be removed in order to form a large room where a party of Guns could have lunch when shooting in the vicinity.

Lodges built for head keepers, particularly on very large estates, might also contain a suite of two or three comfortably furnished bedrooms for the purpose of accommodating young bachelor Guns in order to alleviate overcrowding in the mansion when a big shooting party was in residence. Some lodges included a large range of bedrooms, not only for the family and visiting Guns, loaders and gamekeepers, but for boarding single under-keepers who 'lived in' as part of the household.

Gamekeepers' lodges continued to be built on a regular basis, often in an attractive architectural style, right up until the outbreak of the First World War. Following the cessation of hostilities in 1918, changing financial circumstances caused by increased taxation, forced the majority of landowners to scale down their shooting operations, resulting in far fewer gamekeepers being employed. Many keepers' lodges subsequently fell into disrepair, were sold off by estates or let out to tenants, or were used to accommodate farm staff.

Details of the gamekeepers' lodges listed in the sales prospectus for the Lilleshall Abbey estate, Shropshire, 1917:

The Head Keeper's Lodge, home of Mr F.B. Causton, head gamekeeper to the Duke of Sutherland:
'…situated near the Abbey – brick built and tiled, and containing entrance lobby, two sitting rooms, gun room, kitchen and four bedrooms, with the following out offices – scullery, dairy, two store houses, five kennels, two stall stable, cow shed for two, and ditto for four, trap house, two pig-sties, fowl houses, and good garden extending to .873 acres, 3 rods and 20 perches.'

Double Gates' Lodge, home of John Grass, an under-keeper:
'An "improved" lodge, of brick construction, with stone dressing, black and white gables and tiled roof, containing a porch, entrance lobby, parlour, kitchen, scullery, larder, three bedrooms, coal house, tool store, and an earth closet.'

'Cambridge Hill'; the head keeper's lodge at Six Mile Bottom during the Edwardian period
(courtesy of W G Barton)

The fall and rise of the keepers' lodge

The future of the traditional gamekeepers' lodge was dealt a further blow after the end of World War Two in 1945, when new regulations recommended the provision of running water and flushable lavatories in all properties. Rather than go to the expense of installing these facilities in old lodges in isolated locations, a large number of estates simply abandoned the lodges and built new red brick utilitarian agricultural workers' houses near mains services in order to accommodate their gamekeepers.

Over the past half century or so, many historic keepers' lodges have been bought, modernised and turned into attractive homes, thus ensuring the survival of a large number of architectural gems. Indeed at the present time, 'Keeper's Lodge' or 'Keeper's Cottage' is often a much sought after address amongst the professional and business classes, and frequently boasts amenities such as a swimming pool, a tennis court or a granny flat!

Gate-house lodges

Originating from manorial gate-houses where they were constructed to house a gate-keeper or even soldiers as security, lodges at the entrance to grand country houses came to the fore in Georgian times and, owing to the love of symmetry at the time, they might well have been built in pairs – one either side of the driveway. A lodge-keeper, possibly an old retainer who was past retiring age, would have lived there and was generally expected to be on hand at any time of the day or night in order to open and close the main gates on the arrival and exit of carriages and horses containing their employer, his family and friends.

Gate lodges were often quite ornate, but none more so than the one built at the entrance to the Dromana Estate in Co. Waterford, Ireland. Looking more like the Brighton Pavilion than a lodge, it comprises a central pointed archway, at the top of which is an onion-shaped dome and is, overall, a strange combination of Gothic and exotic Eastern styles.

Just inside Greenwich Park in London stands the lodge built in 1851 for the keeper of the park. Designed by John Phipps, it has multi-coloured brickwork, a roof of alternating plain and fish-scale tiles and a timber jetty and Tudor-style beams at the front.

Somewhat 'fairytale' in appearance is the 'Old Lodge' at Leigh in Kent. It was originally part of Hall Place which underwent major reconstruction in 1870 when the property was bought by Samuel Morley for the sum of £42,000 – and the deer herd for £230! Morley went on to become the Governor of the Bank of England (1903–05) and was created the 1st Baron Hollenden. Far more formal and dignified is the entrance to the Fonthill estate in Wiltshire where the gate lodge forms an archway over the drive. Owned by Lord Margadale, the estate comprises outstanding gardens, farms, forestry, a stud, plus some spectacular pheasant and partridge shooting.

A fairytale gate lodge at Leigh, Kent

The gate lodge at Fonthill (*courtesy of C G Hallam*)

Lodges as meeting places

'Lodges' of any description have always been a place to which men could escape from day to day life. One only has to look at Masonic lodges to realise this. They did though, actually begin life in medieval times as an on-site workshop and a mason's lodge would have been constructed just as soon as work started… and dismantled once the main project was complete. This concept of a 'lodge' was eventually adopted by Freemasons and similar societies. They were (and still are in certain cases) residences and/or meeting places where women were most definitely not encouraged. Bearing in mind what might have gone on in some of the most male-orientated places, there were obvious good reasons for the exclusion of wives, mothers and other females of a delicate disposition!

Supposedly a religious organisation, the Order of the Friars of St Francis of Wycombe, also known as The Hell Fire Club, was the 'brain-child' of Sir Francis Dashwood and met at his Buckinghamshire home between 1749 and 1760.

Rules of the club had him and his friends dress up as the highest order of clergymen before then partaking of far more than tea and biscuits with the vicar! Similar 'clubs' were formed in London, the caves of Wookey Hole in Somerset and, in Ireland, at Montpelier Hill outside Dublin where one of their venues still exists – admittedly in not the best state of repair – in the form of a building officially known as Mount Pelier Lodge but nowadays generally referred to as the 'Hell Fire Club'. Whilst originally built in 1725 as a hunting lodge, it was, between 1735 and 1741, used as a place in which the local gentry could indulge in activities not normally associated with 'the chase' as we know it! Eventually the place was damaged by fire (whether by accident or design is unknown) but its structure still remains – along with a reputation for being haunted.

Mount Pelier Lodge, Ireland – a hunting lodge built in the eighteenth century
which became infamous due to it being the meeting place
of the 'Hell Fire Club'

LOCATION, LOCATION, LOCATION

❦

I T MIGHT SEEM AN OBVIOUS THING TO SAY, but the abundance or otherwise of sporting lodges in certain parts of the country depended upon the quality and quantity of sport likely to be found there! The enterprising Victorian sportsmen who built the great majority of these lodges were not bound by modern day planning constraints so invariably chose sites which gave easy access to shooting, fishing or deer stalking; something then considered to be of more importance than initial travel arrangements. Indeed, in pre-railway days, it often took a sportsman up to a week to reach remote shooting quarters in far flung outposts of the West Country or Scotland, travelling by coach or steamer, or a combination of both.

SCOTLAND

Scotland, without a doubt, has more shooting and fishing lodges than any other part of Great Britain, particularly in the Highland counties of Ross-shire, Sutherland, Inverness-shire and Argyll, all of which were 'opened up' for sport in the mid-nineteenth century following the downturn in large scale sheep farming. Lodges sprang up throughout the Highlands and Islands at this time, sometimes in places more accessible by sea than overland. A surprising number of these lodges still survive today and with the advantage of good road links and, in some cases, helicopter landing facilities, continue to accommodate visiting sportsmen, albeit on a weekly or a fortnightly, rather than a seasonal basis.

Letting out homes as a lodge

Many Scottish lairds made their ancestral homes available for shooting lodge purposes too and accommodated parties of sportsmen in stately, if not always luxurious, conditions. During the mid-Victorian period, the Macleod of Macleod let out his family seat, Dunvegan Castle on the Isle of Skye – together with the associated sporting rights – to a succession of wealthy English tenants. In Ross-shire, Colonel Walter Ross of Cromarty, leased out Cromarty House (situated on the south side of the Cromarty Firth), as a lodge during the season, and in 1904, charged his sporting tenant, Stanley Greville Harding, a London businessman, £85 for the house and £200 for shootings over 7,500 acres…said to yield an average annual bag of '1 or 2 stags, a few roe deer, 40 grouse, 30 black game, 600 partridges, 30 pheasants, 50 woodcock, 500 pigeons, 80 or 90 hares and 3,000 rabbits.' In Ayrshire, John Campbell Kennedy of Dunure rented out Dalquharran Castle, his modernised Robert Adam castle-style mansion, which boasted seventeen bedrooms, gas lighting and a lift – along with a small mixed shoot plus salmon and sea trout fishing in the river Girvan.

The Harding family – tenants of Cromarty House…

Cromarty House in 1904

Accommodating a need

Several major Highland landowners divided up their vast moorland estates into shootings specifically for letting purposes, often building substantial lodges to accommodate their sporting tenants. In the far north of Scotland, the Dukes of Sutherland, who then owned the greater part of the county of Sutherland, created a large number of sporting properties during the mid-Victorian period and constructed a series of lodges in what has become known as the 'Sutherland style', varying in size according to the rental value of the attached shootings, fishings and the corresponding demands of the tenants.

Across the Minch in the Outer Hebrides, Sir James Matheson, owner of the 404,000 acre island of Lewis, laid out a total of twelve sporting estates between 1850 and the time of his death in 1878 – providing dedicated lodge accommodation for many of his properties. Contemporary reports state that Sir James spent a total of £19,289 on the provision of shooting lodges and their attendant offices, which often included a coach house, a stable block, and a substantial slate-roofed gamekeeper's cottage with adjoining gun dog kennels. These imposing edifices were described by a journalist in *The Glasgow Daily Mail* in 1877 as being 'Shooting lodges that catch the eye on the verge of desolation, built by the capital of Sir James or of sportsmen who obtain a long lease on the shootings.'

The Earls of Dunmore, owners of the adjoining island of Harris followed Sir James's example, forming a series of shootings, fishings and deer forests between 1862 and 1883 – again with letting in mind. Later in the 1880s (and early 1890s), both Sir Arthur Campbell-Orde, proprietor of North Uist, and Lady Emily Gordon Cathcart, proprietress of South Uist, Benbecula and Barra, also opened up their island estates to sporting tenants, building shooting lodges and providing hotel accommodation for angling tourists.

In all, a total of 30 sporting estates were formed in the Outer Hebrides between 1850 and 1900, ranging from prestigious deer forests with castle type shooting lodges, to relatively cheap mixed shootings and fishings where accommodation was provided in a small lodge or a dedicated suite of rooms at a local inn. In addition, six comfortable hotels were built at strategic points on the islands, geared specifically to the needs of anglers, each with specially allocated river beats or lochs.

A spreading phenomenon

By the beginning of the Edwardian era shooting lodges could be found as far north as the Orkney and Shetland Islands, although most were lairds' houses that had been made available to the tenants of the various estates. A total of 14 properties were offered for letting purposes throughout the islands at this time, one of the most prestigious being Graemeshall on Mainland Orkney, which boasted a substantial 14 bedroomed house, complete with a private golf course, a tennis court, a chapel seating 35 persons, the exclusive use of two trout lochs and the shootings over 3,000 acres of moorland, said to yield an average annual bag of 200 to 250 red grouse and 200 snipe.

Royal connections

Eastern Scotland boasts a particularly impressive array of shooting lodges, stretching down from Caithness in the far north to the county of Angus on the Firth of Tay. Purpose-built or converted from existing buildings during the Victorian period, these lodges were either opened in order to accommodate sportsmen visiting the many grouse moors and deer forests in the region, or for the benefit of anglers fishing the Thurso, Carron, Spey, Dee, the North and South Esk and numerous other classic salmon and sea trout rivers. Many of the ancestral homes in the eastern counties have also served as summer lodges for sporting tenants at one time and another.

Balmoral Castle on Deeside, undoubtedly one of the grandest of the many shooting lodges to spring up in eastern Scotland, was commissioned by Queen Victoria and Prince Albert in 1853 following their purchase of the 17,400 acre Balmoral estate for the sum of 30,000 guineas. Built in the Scottish 'baronial' style on the site of an existing castle – and of a size sufficient enough to provide ample accommodation for the Royal family, their guests and staff during the sporting season – the house embodied all of the latest modern conveniences of the day. The Royal family subsequently visited Balmoral annually, with Prince Albert and his young sons shooting, fishing and stalking and the Queen and their daughters riding and walking, invariably in the company of John Brown, who was, as is well-known, her favourite ghillie.

Skibo Castle in Sutherland, is another shooting lodge with enviable connections and was built between 1899 and 1901 by the Scottish-American

Skibo House, Sutherland, not long after being built at the turn of the twentieth century

millionaire steel magnate and philanthropist, Andrew Carnegie, one of the world's richest men (who is, incidentally, credited as being the 'father' of the public library system). Surrounded by a 20,000 acre estate, with red, roe and fallow deer, red grouse, black game, pheasants and partridges, all of which abounded on the estate prior to the outbreak of the Great War in 1914, Skibo also had fifteen miles of salmon and sea trout fishings on the river Evelix. Nowadays an exclusive private members' club, Skibo Castle hosted the wedding reception of the singer Madonna and film producer Guy Ritchie in 2000.

Many shooting lodges in eastern Scotland have accommodated members of the royal family, politicians and the rich and famous over the years, especially those in the more remote areas where visits could be made in secrecy and appropriate levels of security maintained.

In the other regions of Scotland, namely central, the south-west and the Borders, sporting tenants and lessees have traditionally stayed in ancestral castles and country houses used for shooting lodge purposes, rather than in purpose-built shooting lodges, which are few and far between.

Perthshire, with its diversity of deer forests, grouse moors and fishings, almost certainly has more shooting lodges than any of the other counties. Lodges tend to be smaller than those found elsewhere in Scotland, particularly those used solely for fishing.

Temporary lodge accommodation

Farm houses, crofts and even manses have also been pressed into service as temporary lodges, particularly in the Highlands and Islands, where the smaller shooting lodges have often required overflow accommodation for bachelor sportsmen, or for anglers fishing on the more distant parts on an estate. In recent years, sporting estates have tended to restore and convert redundant cottages and farmhouses to accommodate sporting tenants, rather than arranging board and lodgings elsewhere. This enables properties to be rented out as holiday cottages outside the sporting season or during un-let periods.

NORTH-EASTERN ENGLAND

Some fairly substantial shooting lodges were also built in north-eastern England during the nineteenth century, specifically for the purpose of accommodating sportsmen visiting grouse moors in the region. A surprising number were located in North Yorkshire, both in the dales and on the moors. Sadly, though, many are no longer used for sporting purposes and are now owned by the Youth Hostels Association, the National Trust or private accommodation providers.

Bransdale Lodge, on the North Yorkshire moors (now a National Trust property), was constructed as a shooting lodge in about 1828 by Charles Duncombe to celebrate his ennoblement as 1st Baron Feversham. Grinton Lodge in the Yorkshire Dales, was erected in 1817 by John Fenton of Doncaster to serve as a shooting quarters for Grinton Moor in Swaledale. Built in the style of a castellated mansion, the lodge later passed to the Charlesworth family of Wakefield, who continued to use it during the grouse season until 1946. In 1948, Grinton was acquired by the present owners, the Youth Hostels Association for use as a youth hostel. In their 1995 Accommodation Guide, they state 'This former shooting lodge retains much of its original character', but also added that the tiled game larder had become the cycle shed!

Cold comfort

Erected at a time when sportsmen were used to living along Spartan lines and servants were plentiful, Yorkshire lodges were commodious but frequently cold and draughty, and would nowadays be most definitely un-suited to modern day living requirements. Improved road facilities have rendered the need for some obsolete, while others have been replaced by much smaller purpose-built lodges or even quite modest houses and bungalows.

It was not uncommon for the more traditional Yorkshire shooting lodges to have, in addition, one or two small shooting boxes situated on the edge of the grouse moor. Constructed of stone, wood or corrugated iron, they served as luncheon accommodation as well as providing a refuge in foul weather and, in some cases, also acted as an assembly point for the Guns if the lodge was located some distance away.

As in Scotland, some existing mansions and hotels were put over to shooting lodge use during the sporting season. The Dukes of Devonshire used Bolton Abbey, their Yorkshire seat, as accommodation when shooting over the Bolton estate moors in Wharfedale whilst the textile magnate and politician, Lord Illingworth, owner of Ramsgill Moor in Nidderdale from 1927 until 1941, chose the Majestic Hotel in Harrogate as a base for himself and his invited guns. Other moorland proprietors or tenants simply lodged in a village inn or a farm house whenever they came to shoot grouse.

A shooting box at Wessenden Head, Marsden, West Yorkshire…also showing the keeper's hut and rearing equipment in the right-hand foreground

THE NORTH-WEST OF ENGLAND

The growth of interest in grouse shooting in the north of England during the mid-nineteenth century resulted in shooting lodges of varying sizes being built in the Lake District counties of Cumberland and Westmoreland, and in the moorland areas of north and eastern Lancashire. Generally smaller than their counterparts in Yorkshire, these lodges were commissioned by local landowners in order to serve remote parts of an estate; provide accommodation for sporting tenants, or, of course, themselves.

Lodges were built in some quite spectacular locations. Skiddaw Lodge (now an independent youth hostel), lies beneath the summit of Skiddaw in the Cumbrian Mountains, approximately 1,550 feet above sea level. The Bungalow near Rampsgill, situated at the head of Martindale in the remote Martindale deer forest in Westmoreland, is a replica of a Tyrolean style shooting lodge erected by Austrian workmen for the lessee, the 5th Earl of Lonsdale, during the Edwardian period and was said to be the 'perfect dwelling for two sportsmen'. March Bank, near Longtown on the English-Scottish border constructed as a shooting lodge in 1850 by Sir Frederick Graham, on a hilltop on his Netherby estate, is now an award-winning country house hotel – which can, however, still arrange shooting and fishing for its guests on the nearby River Esk.

Kelbrook Lodge at Kelbrook in East Lancashire, an Edwardian shooting lodge built in 1908 by Edward Carr, a wealthy lawyer to entertain his clients and friends is still used for sporting purposes. Owned by Michael Meggison, a member of the British Olympic shooting team in 1980 and 1984, the property is home to the Kelbrook Shooting School, which offers superlative tuition and clay pigeon shooting facilities.

Clean living!

Local hostelries occasionally served as temporary shooting lodges in the North-West. In August 1898, the soap magnate, Viscount Leverhulme, took over the Sun Inn at Pooley Bridge on Ullswater to provide accommodation for himself and guests who had been invited to shoot over a nearby grouse moor which he had rented from the Earl of Lonsdale.

Lodge life in the Peak District

Further south, in the Peak District, the development of grouse shooting in the nineteenth century also led to the construction of a number of new shooting lodges and the conversion of some existing buildings into lodges to enable landowners or sporting tenants and lessees to live on their moors in some style during the season. In this instance, lodges were built not only by members of the aristocracy with several estates, but also by wealthy businessmen who had made their fortune in Sheffield in the steel, snuff or cutlery industries and had acquired grouse moors for status purposes.

These lodges were often within easy striking distance of Sheffield, which allowed their owners to commute back and forth to their factories or offices as and when necessary. Stanedge Lodge, for example – probably one of the most isolated houses within the Sheffield city boundary – was re-constructed from an earlier property by Sheffield lawyer and

A well managed moor – and a well maintained line of butts. The popularity of grouse shooting meant that wealthy businessmen had conveniently situated lodges built somewhere close at hand

grouse shooting enthusiast, B P Broomhead, in about 1869. It later passed to the Wilson family, Sheffield snuff manufacturers, who in their heyday owned 6,500 acres of moorland, consisting of Stanedge, Bamford and also Moscar, where a record-breaking bag of 503½ brace of grouse were taken on 28 August 1893.

Upgraded properties

Longshaw Lodge – one of the earliest of the purpose built-lodges in the Peak District – was constructed around 1827 by the 5th Duke of Rutland expressly as a shooting base for his moorland estate on the Derbyshire/south Yorkshire border. At the same time he built a total of nine keepers' cottages on the property; thus presumably ensuring that game was adequately preserved and that poachers were kept at bay! Situated at around 1,070 feet above sea level, the lodge is now owned by the National Trust and houses the visitor centre for the Longshaw estate.

Several other old established aristocratic families with moors in the Peak District used their subsidiary country houses to provide lodge accommodation. The Earls Fitzwilliam from Wentworth Woodhouse near Rotherham, upgraded Hallfield House into a combined shooting lodge and gamekeeper's residence in order to serve the Bradfield Moors, while the Harpur-Crewe family of Calke Abbey pressed Warslow Hall, originally the land agent's house, into service as an impromptu lodge for their Alstonefield estate on the Staffordshire-Derbyshire border.

WALES

Shooting lodges began to appear in Wales during the mid-nineteenth century, particularly in the northern and central parts of the country where, as in other parts of the country, grouse shooting was beginning to boom. Some magnificently imposing edifices were built – mainly with money obtained from business activities in Liverpool or Manchester. Indeed, as early as 1861, the sporting writer 'Scrutator' was moved to comment:

> A FEW YEARS AGO shootings might be obtained on very moderate terms, but the Manchester Cotton Lords are now buying up land (in North Wales) in all directions, and the race of old Welsh squires, like that of the North American Indians, is rapidly disappearing from their old hunting grounds.

Thomas Taylor, owner of Grecian Mills at Bolton in Greater Manchester, one of the first cotton barons to boast a sporting property in Wales, built Penmaenucha Hall at Penmaenpool in Merionethshire in 1860 to serve as a lodge for his newly acquired estates at Penmaenucha and Arthog. Other businessmen from Lancashire, the West Midlands and London followed suit, either purchasing estates or leasing shooting rights in the north of the Principality over the next few decades and building suitable houses in which to entertain their shooting and fishing guests.

Perhaps the most impressive of all the North Wales lodges, Gwyltha Hiraethog, was built on the Denbighshire moors in 1908 by the millionaire London businessman and Liberal M.P, Hudson Ewbanke Kearley, later 1st Viscount Devonport. A Jacobean style mansion with eleven principal bedrooms and two secondary bedrooms, along with attendant servants' quarters, it was claimed, at 496 metres above sea level, to be the highest inhabited house in Wales and afforded luxury accommodation for the owner whenever he and his guests came to shoot driven grouse over his 7,000 acres of leased moorland. Sadly now in ruins, the lodge once hosted Liberal Prime Minister Lloyd George who stood on the balcony and addressed a large crowd of local people.

Elsewhere in Wales, in the southern, western and parts of the central counties, where walked-up rough shooting was the order of the day and apart from at Margam Abbey, Glanusk, Powis Castle and a handful of other large country estates with intensively keepered driven shoots where Guns boarded

Guns and guests at Penmaenucha, Merionethshire, November 1911

in the mansion, shooting was generally the exclusive preserve of the local squire or the farming tenant and any guests lived in as part of the family. Shooting was also available on a residential basis at a number of hotels (at moderate terms!) during the first half of the twentieth century. As an example, in the 1930s, the Lake Hotel at Llangammarch Wells in Breconshire served as a shooting lodge offering clients the choice of four grouse moors and 2,000 acres of rough shooting, as well as 'fifteen miles of carefully preserved trout fishing'.

THE MIDLANDS AND EAST ANGLIA

Unlike areas that have already been discussed, purpose-built residential shooting lodges are rarely found in the Midlands: principally due to the fact that, in times past, landowners in the region kept the sporting rights over their property in-hand for personal use. In Shropshire, on the Stiperstones and in the surrounding area, where walked-up grouse shooting was let out prior to the Great War, annual sporting tenants invariably stayed in local hotels for the duration of their visit.

The 'Shires' were, arguably, better-known for their hunting rather than shooting opportunities. Hounds meeting at an unknown location

The Midlands was, of course, far better famed for its hunting opportunities and, during Victorian and Edwardian times, it was not uncommon for wealthy foxhunting enthusiasts to own ' hunting boxes ' in fashionable East Midland towns such as Melton Mowbray, thus enabling them to ride to hounds on an almost daily basis during the season (of which much more later). Many of these folk undoubtedly went shooting as guests on local estates during any spare time their principal sport might leave them!

EAST ANGLIA

East Anglia, in contrast, boasts a small, but interesting selection of shooting lodges; ranging from palatial mansions to small cottages used by stalkers and wildfowlers. In addition, Elveden, Sandringham and a number of other great houses in Norfolk and Suffolk which regularly hosted large driven shoots, were refurbished and extended during the Victorian period to provide high quality 'lodge' accommodation for the owners and their guests when they were in residence during the season.

Kelling Hall near Holt in Norfolk – possibly the most ostentatious of all the East Anglian lodges – was built in the Arts and Crafts style in 1914 as a shooting lodge by the Dutch industrialist, Sir Henri Deterding, founder of the Royal Dutch Shell oil company. Designed to be the centre-piece of a large sporting estate, the property was constructed specifically for entertaining shooting parties in the lap of luxury, with thirteen bedrooms, a trophy room and the latest mod cons. In 2008, Sir Henri's descendants put the lodge and the surrounding estate on the market with a price tag of £25 million.

At the other end of the scale, Ketts Oak, a gothic style gamekeeper's house built on the Ryston estate in Norfolk, whilst relegated to the lowly status of a keeper's shed in the 1960s, nevertheless began a new life in the 1990s as an overnight lodge for deer stalkers!

Given the tradition of high quality game shooting in the region, it is unsurprising that East Anglia has some wonderful country hotels which have provided 'lodge' accommodation for shooters ever since the Victorian period. Wildfowling visitors have also been well catered for in small inns and farmhouses (although, given the irregular hours that it entails, some fowlers have traditionally happily bedded down in small wooden huts, caravans or even houseboats to be as near the coast as possible in order to get the best out of their sport).

King of Essex!

Although not built specifically as a shooting lodge, the very well appointed Champion Lodge near Maldon in Essex, seat of the de Crespigny family, was used for this purpose during the 'reign' of Sir Claude Champion de Crespigny, Bt., from 1867 to 1935. Known widely as the 'uncrowned king of Essex', this larger than life character devoted much of his time to wildfowling on the local marshes, fox hunting and shooting on his estate.

With every good wish for Christmas and the New Year.

From Sir Claude and Lady Champion de Crespigny.

Champion Lodge – the seasonal home of Sir Claude Champion de Crespigny, 'the uncrowned king of Essex'!

SOUTHERN ENGLAND

Other than a number of historic lodges connected with former royal hunting grounds, some of which later became country houses and were used to accommodate shooting parties at various times during the nineteenth and twentieth centuries, purpose-built shooting lodges are rarely found in the southern counties of England; in fact, a Hampshire property agent says that 'in forty years in the business, he has never come across a purpose-built residential shooting lodge anywhere in the county.' A lack of need for such buildings is undoubtedly due to the rail links which were established between London and the south coast during the mid-Victorian period (and passed through numerous towns and villages), enabling sportsmen to travel to many districts within the space of a couple of hours, spend a day shooting or fishing, then return to town by express train in time for a late dinner!

Arne House

Arne House, situated on the Isle of Purbeck side of Poole Harbour in Dorset, is one of the few dedicated shooting lodges to be built in the south of England and was erected during the mid-nineteenth century by the Earl of Eldon. Throughout the shooting season he regularly travelled from his country seat,

Arne House, Poole, Dorset; built as a shooting lodge in the mid-1800s
(*courtesy of C G Hallam*)

Encombe House, some seven miles distant, to shoot at Arne or to go wildfowling on the shores of the harbour. According to Don Ford, whose father, Cyril, was gamekeeper at Arne from 1934 until 1940, Arne House (known locally as the 'Shooting Lodge'), was used as a holiday home by a London solicitor throughout this time and the shoot let out to a syndicate. The property suffered from bomb damage during World War Two but has since been restored and extended to provide a substantial residence (although it no longer forms a part of the Arne estate).

Wrackleford, Dorset

Oliver Pope's family has been game shooting at Wrackleford for a century or more. Originally it would have been a day's trek to go up 'on the hill' for shooting, so a pre-fabricated hunting hut was purchased from the Bath and West Show when it came to Dorchester in 1881. The original building was made up of two basic rooms, purposely not internally connected so that it could be used for overnight accommodation if need be.

In keeping with how lodges originate and then progress, in 1990, it was decided that the old 'Shooting Box' needed extending and so the new lodge was built. According to Oliver, 'The new lodge is Tardis-like, and features the main shoot room with its huge circular elm table … Excessively eccentric in one corner is a tower – a spiral staircase takes you up to a little Rapunzel single bedroom, and below is the sunken "Admiral's Well" – a circular seating area with a small coal stove – copied from an Equadorian admiral we knew from his Pacific coast house! The large double doors from the main shoot room lead out to the terrace area and fantastic views facing directly south to Hardy's Monument which overlooks the sea at Abbotsbury …'

The rest of the building is made up of several bedrooms, beaters' room, and a snooker room with its three-quarter size table – and lots of open fireplaces.

Teffont Magna, Wiltshire

Not all that far down the road from Wrackleford is Edward Waddington's 2,600 acre shoot at Teffont Magna. Considered by some to be 'one of Wiltshire's best-kept secrets'; the shoot was voted one of Britain's top twenty best shoots by *Shooting Gazette* magazine. *GunsonPegs*, 'the UK's number one shoot finder' describe it thus: 'Exciting driven red legs and greys. Excellent shoot lodge and hospitality. All days run by enthusiastic owner. Drinks and canapes mid morning, followed by Cordon Bleu lunch in a charming converted barn.' It is the latter fact that interests in this particular instance and the star attraction of the barn – apart from the magnificent traditional country house style dining room – is the shoot lounge which is reminiscent of an Edwardian smoking room, complete with comfortable sofas, sporting paintings, stuffed 'trophies of the chase' and an assortment of quirky antiques!

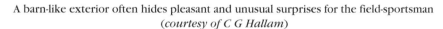

A barn-like exterior often hides pleasant and unusual surprises for the field-sportsman
(*courtesy of C G Hallam*)

THE WEST COUNTRY

In Somerset and Devon, a number of sporting lodges were built during the nineteenth century, not only to accommodate shooters, but also anglers and hunting enthusiasts who came down from London and elsewhere in pursuit of stag, fox and otter in areas such as Exmoor and Dartmoor.

Watersmeet House near Lynmouth – situated in the Watersmeet Valley at the confluence of the East Lyn River and Hoar Oak water – is one of the earliest Exmoor lodges and was built in 1832 as a dual-purpose fishing and shooting lodge by the Reverend Walter Halliday, the son of a wealthy London banker. In the centre of Exmoor, John Knight (a wealthy Worcestershire ironmaster who, in 1818, had purchased the Royal Forest of Exmoor from the Crown for the sum of £50,000), turned Simonsbath House – constructed originally in the seventeenth century to house the deputy-forester – into a shooting and hunting lodge. He laid out a deer park, which he then stocked with fallow deer and also provided a circular shooting tower as a 'hide' from where he could shoot the deer. Knight is also known for his abortive attempt to introduce red grouse to Exmoor during the1820s.

The Cleeve, delightfully located at Porlock, Somerset, was known to have been purpose-built as a hunting lodge during Victorian times; sadly, for whom it was constructed is not clear – nor is when it ceased being used for its original function (but, according to the current owners, most likely sometime prior to 1930). However, it thrives today as an extremely luxurious self-catering holiday let which can sleep up to twenty-eight guests.

The Cleeve was originally built during the Victorian period in order to take advantage of the hunting on offer around Porlock, Somerset…

…the magnificent fireplace must have heard many stories and warmed the cold bones of many a sportsman and woman! (*both photos courtesy of Kevin Brambill*)

An all-round sportsman

On the southern fringes of Exmoor at Morebath, Henry Grey Thornton, a member of the Thornton banking dynasty, built Warmore House as his shooting lodge around 1900 – complete with modern sanitation, stabling for his hunters and a gun room. An all-round sportsman (he was also honorary secretary of the Culmstock Otter Hounds), Thornton acquired fishing rights on a stretch of the river Exe and established a small pheasant shoot on land surrounding the house. His game book for 1901 records that in one thirteen day period between the 18th and the 30th January, while in residence at Warmore House, he went out fox hunting once, rode out with the Devon and Somerset Staghounds twice, travelled to Burnham-on-Sea for a hare coursing meeting once, fished for grayling in the river Exe once, and spent two days shooting pheasants, rabbits and woodcock.

Somewhere to stay

Country inns and hotels on Exmoor started to cater for sportsmen in a big way during the nineteenth century and, as elsewhere in the country, they offered their clients shooting lodge type facilities. The Carnarvon Arms at Dulverton, built adjacent to Dulverton railway station in 1874, seduced potential guests with the promise of trout and salmon fishing on the Rivers Exe and Barle and also a stable of good hireling hunters and hacks for those interested in stag and fox hunting. The Exmoor White Horse Hotel at Exford, also catered for hunting folk, and, in 1923, was rented in its entirety as a hunting box by Mr Algernon Heber-Percy of Hodnet Hall, Shropshire, when he took over the mastership of the Quarme Harriers for a couple of seasons. The Crown Hotel, another Exford hotel, not only provided horse hire facilities and free fishing, but also rough shooting over 500 acres. Many Exmoor hotels and guest houses continue the sporting hospitality tradition today.

Fishing, hunting, shooting and sloe gin!

Several country inns and farmhouses on Dartmoor also provided lodge type accommodation for sportsmen, usually bachelors of independent, but limited means. In the halcyon days of the Edwardian era, they were quite likely to spend the entire shooting and fishing season on the moor, having first purchased an annual Duchy of Cornwall shooting licence for ten shillings (50p) and a one pound ten shillings (£1.50p) rod licence which permitted them to catch salmon, sea trout and other fish anywhere on the East and West Dart rivers (as well as their tributaries).

The Two Bridges Hotel at Two Bridges, then known as The Saracen's Head and kept by Henry Trinaman, was a favoured haunt of these men, frequently hardy characters, addicted to whisky or sloe gin, who came to fish for salmon and sea trout on the Dart, to shoot snipe, teal, rabbits or black game, or to follow the Dartmoor or the Lamerton Foxhounds, the harriers, or the otter hounds if they happened to be hunting in the area.

The Two Bridges Hotel on Dartmoor (formerly known as The Saracen's Head) was a favoured resting place for all who wished to hunt, shoot and fish

Grouse shooting lodges on Dartmoor?

Traditionally associated with fishing and hunting rather than game shooting, Dartmoor could well have been sprinkled with shooting lodges had the red grouse introduction experiments carried out prior to the Great War been a success. Indeed, one anonymous journalist went as far as predicting that Dartmoor bound 'grouse trains' full of shooters would eventually steam out of Waterloo and Paddington in the same manner as those heading for the north of England and Scotland! Sadly, the experiment was doomed to failure due to unsuitable environmental conditions – although, according to sources, the birds are still present in very small numbers in some of the more remote areas.

Endsleigh

Endsleigh is undoubtedly one of the most prestigious of the few lodges that can be found in this part of the world. Situated on the banks of the river Tamar on the south-western edge of Dartmoor, it was built in 1812 as a combined shooting and fishing lodge by Georgina, 6th Duchess of Bedford in order that she and her family could live in some style on the 22,000 acre Bedford Tavistock estate during the sporting season. Designed by the well known architect, Sir Jeffry Wyattville as a *cottage ornée*, with gardens laid out by Humphry Repton, the lodge was used only once a year when the Bedfords arrived from Woburn along with their pets, a retinue of servants and a selection of the family silver. Now a Grade 1 listed building, Endsleigh is today a luxury country house hotel, owned by Olga Polizzi.

Endsleigh, south-west Dartmoor, was built by Georgina, Duchess of Bedford as a combined shooting and fishing lodge. Today it is a wonderful hotel loved by all who visit. The gardens were laid out by Humphry Repton – and are no doubt much enjoyed nowadays by the hotel guests (*courtesy of Helen Costello/Hotel Endsleigh*)

West Country lodges for the 21st Century

In addition to the various old established shooting and fishing lodges in the West Country – and the rural hotels and inns that have provided residential accommodation for visiting sportsmen since the Victorian period – in recent years, a number of new lodges have been opened to cater for modern day sportsmen who patronise the commercial high pheasant shoots which have become a part and parcel of the local shooting scene, particularly in Devon and Somerset.

Loyton Lodge at Morebath on Exmoor, for example, was renovated and converted from a range of courtyard buildings in 2003, and can accommodate up to twenty guests in luxurious surroundings, offering both shooting and 'country house' type breaks, complete with bar facilities and gourmet food prepared and cooked by the in-house chef, Nick Pyle. At Maristow situated on the south-west edge of Dartmoor, the historic Maristow Barton farmhouse has been transformed into a five-star shooting lodge by owner Clive Jacobs to provide de-luxe accommodation for guests on the 6,500 acre Maristow shoot. It apparently benefits from a secure gunroom, WiFi internet facilities and lunch menus designed by celebrity chef, John Burton-Race.

Loyton Lodge, Morebath, Exmoor
(*courtesy of Alick Barnes/Loyton Lodge*)

IRELAND

Shooting lodges were erected in various parts of Ireland during the nineteenth century; particularly in the counties of Galway and Mayo on the Atlantic coast – which boasted excellent fishing, rough shooting and wildfowling. Many were built by landed proprietors in order that they could shoot and fish on distant or detached parts or their estate, or to let to tenants together with associated sporting rights. Others were constructed by rich businessmen who had purchased or leased land for sporting purposes and needed a comfortable base in which to stay when shooting or fishing.

Fairies and opera singers!

Construction work on Shean Lodge in Co. Mayo, one of the first purpose built shooting and fishing lodges in Ireland, began in 1843 but, according to local folklore, was put on hold for around a year until the landowner, Major Bellingham, agreed not to tamper with, or remove a ' fairy rock ' which obstructed the view from the property. The lodge and associated fishings on the Owenduff River were later acquired by the eminent Dublin surgeon, Seton Pringle, F.R.C.S.I., who, in 1939, rented it to the world renowned Irish tenor, Count John McCormack. Shean passed to the current owners, the Craigie family of Dublin in the 1940s and continues to operate as a sporting lodge, offering salmon and sea trout fishing and other activities to residential guests.

Burrishoole Lodge – like Shean Lodge – is another nineteenth century Mayo shooting lodge and stands on a promontory at the Newport end of Clew Bay. It once offered its tenants salmon and sea trout fishing, seal shooting and rough shooting over 5,000 acres but eventually became the home of Ernie O'Malley, the Irish revolutionary turned writer. Aasleagh Lodge (also in Mayo), was rented as a fishing lodge in the 1970s by Countess Mountbatten of Burma and her husband, Lord Brabourne (it now belongs to the Fisheries Board). Fermoyle Lodge in Co. Galway, built by the Berridge family in 1875 and still the hub of a thriving sporting estate in the 1930s, currently houses the Nicola Stronach Art Gallery and offers bed and breakfast accommodation while Mountain Lodge, in the Galtee Mountains in Co. Tipperary, is a circular-shaped shooting lodge formerly owned by Lady Beatrice Pole-Carew and Lady Constance Butler but which has since become a youth hostel.

A lady wears the breeches

Mountain Lodge in Co. Monaghan, is another Irish lodge with a claim to fame, situated some ten miles from Rossmore Castle, seat of the Lords Rossmore, the building was constructed during the nineteenth century in order to accommodate members of the family when visiting their 10,000 acre grouse moor. In this instance, the 5th Lord Rossmore broke new ground in the 1890s by employing a lady gamekeeper on the property. Ann Holland is credited as being Ireland's first ever female keeper: a crack-shot, Mrs Holland quickly stopped all poaching activities in the district after shooting the heel off the boot of a fleeing poacher with her old police carbine!

Hotels as a sporting home from home

For those unable to rent a lodge and sporting rights on a seasonal basis, suitable hotels were available throughout Ireland from the mid-nineteenth century onwards. Offering residential angling and shooting facilities for a week or more at a time, in some instances, the quality of the sport apparently left a lot to be desired. Many hotels also catered for members of the hunting fraternity, hiring out hacks and hunters and providing livery stabling.

The Clonwyn Hotel at Portumna in Co.Galway, was typical of many small Irish sporting hostelries and offered their guests free trout and pike fishing, rough shooting and wildfowling at an 'all in' price of £3. 13s.06d (less than £3.75p) per week during the 1930s – and all that with ghillie and dog hire as an optional extra! The owners also offered to arrange 'hunter hire' from the local stables. Mongan's Hotel at Carna in Co. Galway, was a much larger establishment and, in addition to 'electric light and running water', provided their guests with a choice of free trout fishing, sea fishing and rough shooting over 60,000 acres - unlike the Clonwyn, however, they did not specify weekly charges in their advertising literature of the time.

1938 advertisement extolling the virtues of fishing in Ireland!

An advert from The Field *dated 18 September, 1858*

SHOOTING AND FISHING IN THE WEST OF IRELAND – To be let for 7 or 14 years, the exclusive right to shoot over 15,000 acres of good grouse shooting, with snipe, woodcock and wildfowl in the season, together with some first-rate salmon and sea trout fishing, with an excellent comfortable furnished lodge, containing dining and drawing room, six bedrooms, independent servants apartments, with all necessary domestic offices and outbuildings. Land sufficient for 5 or 6 cows can be let with the lodge.

Apply 'Anon' (No 1299) Field Office, London.

Ireland – and in particular, Southern Ireland is, as has been shown above, the perfect place to indulge in any sporting pastime. It is, of course, particularly well-known for its fox hunting as portrayed in the late nineteenth and early twentieth century books of Anglo-Irish writers Somerville and Ross (and subsequent Channel 4 1980s adaptations of *The Irish R M*). Even today, the names of packs such as 'The Galway Blazers' cannot fail to excite the imagination of anyone and everyone who aspires to hunt in the fashion as was once common throughout the British Isles.

HUNTING BOXES

Some would argue that a hunting 'lodge' and a hunting 'box' were two entirely separate things: according to one particular estate agent, '…a lodge was often part of a large estate, and was purpose-built with stables and formal entertaining rooms' whereas hunting boxes '…with a couple of bedrooms and a large dining room table (were) perfect for those living in London who wanted a weekend base in the country.' Whether one agrees with that distinction or not, there are very definite reasons for where hunting lodges and/or boxes were located.

The first part of the 1800s is frequently described as being the 'heyday of hunting' when the sport went from being a mainly private affair enjoyed by a select few – usually titled – landowners, to one financed by subscription and attended by many of the rural and urban-based middle classes. The railways helped as it was possible for those from far away to travel and hunt with what eventually became known as the 'Shire' packs of the Quorn, Cottesmore, Belvoir, Fernie and Pytchley where some of the best fox-hunting was to be found. Some might possibly have travelled there and back in a day, but a great many more preferred to stay for a week or more… and so the 'hunting box' was developed.

High society and fashionable meets

Despite the name, there was nothing 'box-like' about many of these properties: such a place near Melton Mowbray which is nowadays a private house and the owners wish it not to be identified, was built with eight bedrooms and had all the trappings of a London residence.

Owners of the time entertained with regularity (one particular property became known as 'Claret Lodge' because of the vast quantity of wine consumed there) and, in Melton, those who were there all winter for the hunting, were joined by many of London's high society – in fact, it is reckoned that it was here rather than London, where much of Edward, Prince of Wales' courtship of Mrs Wallis Simpson took place. Those who didn't own a hunting box of their own would often rent properties for the season, but it was important to get in there quick as otherwise only places well away from the majority of meets would be available for rent. Charles Richardson (hunting editor of *The Field* at the time), writing *The Complete Foxhunter* in 1908, had this to say on the matter:

MELTON MOWBRAY is undoubtedly the best and most popular centre, because four of the Shire packs are within easy reach, and it is possible to hunt on six days of the week, without, except perhaps on Thursday, having to go very long distances to covert. On Monday and Friday the Quorn is chiefly patronised by those hunting from Melton. On Tuesday the Cottesmore are generally handy, and on Wednesday the Belvoir are in the Croxton Park country, and seldom meet more than half a dozen miles from the town sacred to foxhunting and pork pies.

Thursday is as a rule the most difficult day of the week. The Cottesmore and Mr. Fernie's hounds are both out...but meeting them often involves a somewhat long journey to covert. The Quorn do not profess to hunt on Thursdays, but frequently have a bye-day, and all the Quorn country can be reached from Melton by anyone who is determined to get all the sport he can. Friday has already been alluded to...while on Saturday the Meltonian hunts with the Belvoir or Cottesmore, and as a rule one or other of these packs meet close to Melton on this day.

Hunting in the Midlands has always been seen as fashionable – and a place for fashion

In his book *The Keen Foxhunter's Miscellany* (Quiller 2010), author Peter Holt recounts the tale of a Melton Mowbray hunting box, a horse and a bet which took place during the latter half of the nineteenth century. The bet was made by a fellow named Peter Flower, who 'wagered that he could ride a horse up the staircase to the first floor of the hunting lodge he shared with his two brothers. Flower galloped his huge bay up the stairs to the landing. All very good. But nothing would induce the creature to come down again. This was after dinner on a Saturday night. The horse stayed there all day Sunday. It was not until Monday morning that workmen were available to construct a platform so that the horse could be lowered to the ground by ropes. The hunter was subsequently sold to Irish peer Lord Annaly who renamed him First Flight.'

Hunting boxes in other locations

Elsewhere, certain areas of the country were every bit as popular. Charles Richardson further opined on the subject of hunting boxes in and around Delamere Forest, Cheshire: 'All about the forest are hunting-boxes, varying from the mansion in a park to the pretty roadside cottage, the stabling of which at times makes a bigger block of buildings than the house itself.'

When talking of hunting in North Yorkshire he mentions that:

> FOR MANY YEARS 'the Bridge', as Catterick Bridge is called locally, was a most popular place with hunting visitors, and at one time it was no easy matter to obtain quarters at the hotel, so great was the demand. The hotel in question was originally one of the several hunting boxes which Lord Darlington caused to be built in his huge country, and the big room in which the hunting visitors dined has the arms of the Vane family carved on the ceiling. But unfortunately the house is no longer a hotel – although it is understood that accommodation can still be secured, and there is still a vast range of stabling.

After making enquiries during the course of research for this book, it seems that the hotel is once more just that. Tina Birnie, the current licencee of the Bridge House Hotel, says that, 'there is a Coat of Arms in the ceiling of the present bar and also on the wall of the restaurant, and I understand from things I have read and heard from the locals that people did used to stay here for the fishing, hunting, and racing of course which is still active today.' Apparently, around the time of which Charles Richardson wrote, the place was being 'used as a private summer house for the fishing' – presumably the reason he commented that it was no longer a hotel.

Before leaving Mr Richardson's most informative and charming book, there is, among its pages, a seemingly random photo included – to which there is no mention made within the text! It shows what the caption claims to be 'The Comte de Madie's movable hunting box'… whether the photo was taken abroad (given the owner's name, possibly France?) or in Britain there is no clue…neither is there any indication as to how 'movable' this particular edifice might be – from the photograph, it looks pretty substantial!

The Comte de Madie's movable hunting box

Prices then and now

Returning briefly to Melton Mowbray; in 1929, Egerton Lodge, which was, until that time, a hunting box owned by the Earls of Wilton, was put on the market and subsequently bought by the town estate for £500. The ornamental gardens were eventually to be turned into 'Memorial' gardens, in honour of the victims in both World Wars.

It seems that, always assuming one can be found for sale, a hunting box will nowadays cost the purchaser far more than £500! In Devon recently, a hunting lodge in Lamerton country had a price tag of £2.35 million, whilst up in Scotland at the same time, a property used as a base for hunting with the Buccleuch and Lauderdale (but from where you could also catch salmon at the bottom of the garden!) was on the market for £1.75 million. A contemporary report in the property section of *The Telegraph* newspaper pointed out that properties in good hunting country undoubtedly command a significant premium, even in a period of recession. An agent interviewed for the piece commented: 'It's amazing how many people call up and say they must be in such-and-such Hunt country rather than a particular town or station.'

FISHING HUTS

Other than in the wildest of places, trout and salmon fishing is relatively easy to access and doesn't generally necessitate trekking over such great distances that overnight accommodation might be required; hence the reason that properties built with this objective in mind are less in number than are shooting and stalking lodges – and, therefore, are more difficult to locate. There are though, throughout Britain, a multitude of small fishing huts for daytime use in which the angler can rest, eat his sandwiches or simply contemplate his flies!

A fishing shelter on the Test, Hampshire

The Victorian fishing hut at Bossington, Hampshire (*courtesy of Howard Taylor*/www.upstreamdryfly.com)

The origins of the fishing huts, pavilions…call them what you will…have been already mentioned elsewhere, but the reasons why they are where they are, must surely belong here. It is, most obviously, to do with the quality and abundance of fish to be found in the wild and because of this, many of the 'daily' fishing huts to be found in the south are located along the banks of famous chalk streams such as the Test and Itchen. In the north it seems that the salmon-fishers might be made of stronger stuff as shelters and resting places for them on rivers such as the Tweed, Tay and Dee are far less plentiful.

On large private estates throughout the land, countless landowners showed off their wealth and status by either having lakes dug or diverting existing rivers so that they might form a part of a landscape to be seen from the main house. Despite being but a stone's throw away from home, it seems that some form of fishing lodge was a prerequisite – and the more fancy and ornate, the better.

A picturesque pavilion

As an example of the above, at Alresford in Essex, at what is variously and somewhat confusingly referred to as Alresford Hall, Quarters House, or The Quarters, there is a Chinese fishing temple which was built in 1772 for Colonel Redbow. Originally, it was constructed (for the princely sum of £343 13s 4d) with a veranda over the water and the main room was octagonal in shape. The veranda has long since gone and today the internal appearance of the room is that of a square – due to the fact that the octagonal corners have been altered so as to include hidden cupboards in which fishing tackle can be kept. Although primarily for the use of fishermen, this extremely picturesque pavilion (it featured in a painting by John Constable) was also frequently used as a summer house and a place for intimate banquets and picnics.

Charles Cotton's Fishing House

On a secluded stretch of the River Dove on the Derbyshire/Staffordshire border, stands a charming stone fishing hut built in 1674. Over its door (and at either side of the mantelpiece) is carved a cipher of two entwined letters: one a 'C', the other a 'W'. The W stands for Walton as in 'the father of all fishermen', Izaak Walton and the C for Charles Cotton who had the hut (sometimes referred to as a 'cottage') built near to his home Beresford Hall as a refuge for the times when fishing on this particular part of the river.

Charles Cotton was an English poet and writer born in 1630 and his

Fishing on the River Dove – and shelter offered by the seventeenth century stone hut built by
Charles Cotton – has been enjoyed by many since Izaak Walton's day

piscatorial-based friendship with Izaak Walton began when he (Cotton) was
about twenty-five years of age. However, as writer Graham Downing noted in
his erudite article in *The Field* in 2010, 'Whether Walton himself visited the
fishing house after it had been completed is not known: he would have been
eighty-one years old and the journey from Winchester where he lived, to what
was then a remote part of England would have been long and arduous'.

Referred to in Walton's the *Compleat Angler* (a section of which was actually
written by Cotton), this particular stretch of the Dove offered perfect fishing
and was, therefore, the ideal place to construct such a long-lasting edifice in
which countless generations of fishermen have rested, eaten and talked. That

Cotton's unique fishing house still exists in such fine
fettle is due in no small part to the time, effort and
finances of the present owner, Michael Collins, who
has, in recent years, refurbished the roof and ensured
that it will be around for future generations of fly-
fishermen to enjoy.

Ciphers picking out the intertwining initials of Charles Cotton
and Izaak Walton can still be seen carved in the stone above the
fishing hut's door (*both photos courtesy of Graham Downing*)

Board (masters) and lodgings!

Scotland is famed throughout the world for its fishing hotels, which have provided salmon, sea trout and brown trout angling facilities for clients from all walks of life since the Victorian period. In bygone days these establishments frequently acted as lodges for wealthy 'bachelor anglers' who booked-in for the entire fishing season, arriving a day or to before the start and departing just after the close. It was not unusual for such anglers to be looked after by a 'board master'; a long standing semi-resident guest, who, with the blessing of the proprietor or the manager, allocated guests to their place on the daily fishing roster and gave advice to newcomers! The more prestigious of these old-time Scottish sporting hotels often had a small shoot attached and could arrange stalking on a local estate (in fact, this tradition continues today, with more and more hotels offering shooting and deer stalking in addition to fishing).

Welsh waters

Ease of road access to South and West Wales via the M4, M5 and M50 motorways during the second half of last century has enabled anglers from the Midlands and the Home Counties to visit their favourite river for a day at a time. Despite that fact, a surprising number of better-off anglers have purchased cottages or houses in riverside villages to use as a 'fishing retreat' in order to spend their week-ends and holidays in pursuit of salmon and trout. Some also use their home as a base to participate in local rough shoots, either private or syndicate based.

In the past, however, many anglers of independent means visited south and west Wales for two or three months annually in order to catch salmon, sea trout and other fish on the Dovey, Teify, Towy, Usk, Wye and their tributaries. To do so, they might well have found lodging in hotels and country inns, some of which owned or leased stretches of nearby river fishing. The more impecunious of these men used a local farm house as their fishing 'lodge', paying a very modest fee for meals and a bed. Indeed, in 1937, local farmer, Dan Price at Glan Wye, provided full-board accommodation in a 'modern house fitted with electric light and a bathroom', with free fishing in the river Wye for the princely sum of 10/6d. (52½ p) per day.

Southern style

The southern counties boast some iconic sporting hotels, which in times past hosted both hunting folk and anglers for lengthy periods of time in 'lodge comfort'. In the 1930s, *The Bull* at Downton in Wiltshire was a Mecca for trout fishing enthusiasts, charging three pounds and three shillings (£3.15) a week for board and lodgings, and five shillings (25p) per day for fishing on the hotel waters on the river Avon. *The Grosvenor Hotel* at Stockbridge in Hampshire, continues to serve as the headquarters of the Houghton Club, the most famous fly fishing club in the world (founded in 1822), and provides the focal point for the club's waters on the river Test. It also houses the organisation's club room.

In the New Forest, country inns and hotels not only catered for hunting tourists who visited the area in pursuit of the fox and the deer, but, before the Second World War, accommodated sportsmen who had purchased a Forest Licence which enabled one to shoot on the open forest with one beater and 'not more than three dogs, only two of which should be running at one time'. Nowadays such licences are only issued to people who live on the Forest and its environs.

SHOOTING LODGES ABROAD

Over the water – and far further than the islands of Britain, it seems that very different sporting lodges abound. In North America, cabins in the 'backwoods' are built specifically as overnight accommodation for sportsmen intent on bringing back the biggest and the best. Depending on the exact location, the target species might vary from deer to turkey; from game birds to bear. No matter what the intended quarry, a place to eat, sleep and drink beer seems to be a prerequisite! Most often constructed from beams and slab-wood hacked from the forest, shooting lodges here resemble the archetypal log cabin as portrayed on so many television programmes and films.

A hunting shack in the backwoods of America

Eastern Europe

Bear shooting is not necessarily confined to America – in parts of Eastern Europe, there is still an allocation allowed by the relevant government departments. More common, though, is the pursuit of deer which, in days gone by, would have necessitated the building of a quite grand edifice; the likes of which are now most generally seen as remnants of the past.

As far as deer shooting is concerned, high seats are commonly used. Unlike the basic, open-slatted seats of the UK, some of those in current use in Europe are just a tad more elaborate and are fully enclosed: whilst they might not be quite large enough to contain a double bed and kitchen facilities, they are, however, sufficiently ample so as to be classed as overnight accommodation – and therefore fulfil entirely the dictionary definition of a 'lodge'.

In the Koevsko region of Slovenia, the woodlands are so huge that it is impracticable to enter and hunt on a daily basis, as a result of which most people take advantage of overnight accommodation supplied by the government-run equivalent of the UK's Forestry Commission. Obviously realising the need to bring in much needed finance, the main sporting quarry are wild boar and deer: there is though, for those who wish to aim with nothing more than a camera, the opportunity to 'shoot' at brown bear, lynx and wolf.

A roofed high seat in Slovenia – basic maybe, but used as overnight accommodation by hardy sportsmen on some occasions…

… those less hardy might, though, prefer something a little more substantial in the way of lodgings!

France

Chambord is just one of the many châteaux to be found along the Loire Valley: it is undoubtedly the largest, but though magnificent, perhaps not the prettiest as that honour supposedly goes to the château d'Ussé on the edge of the Chinon forest. In fact, tradition has it that when Charles Perrault, the famous French writer of fairy tales, was looking for a setting for *Sleeping Beauty*, he chose Ussé as his model.

Fairy-tale looks though it might have, Ussé, cannot claim to have been built as a hunting lodge, as is the case with Chambord which was constructed in the sixteenth century purely for that purpose.

Obsessive behaviour

As a young man, François I liked to hunt in the nearby forest of Boulogne and in 1518 he ordered the old castle to be razed in order to make room for a somewhat superior hunting lodge. Several architects put ideas forward and the building constantly changed in design as François adapted the original plans.

There's certainly no doubt as to what this particular king's priorities were: despite his Treasury being empty and he being reduced to raiding the treasuries of the churches, or to melting down his subjects' silver, he insisted that work went on at Chambord. In his enthusiasm for the project, François even proposed to divert the course of the river Loire so that it should flow in front of the château but, in view of the enormity of this task, a smaller river, the Cosson, was chosen instead.

During the peak of its sporting life, Chambord was well stocked with game and there was a great deal of hawking (the Royal Mews once boasted over 300 falcons) and hunting. The resident pack of hounds were extremely well looked after and unrelated bloodlines from other hunting establishments were brought in from all over Europe in order to continually update and improve the Royal strain.

Once the work was eventually completed, François II, Charles IX and Louis XIV were amongst the well-known royals who came frequently to hunt in the forests surrounding Chambord. It is said that Louis XII would take 16ft (5m) ditches on horseback without flinching and that, despite his well-known delicate constitution, Charles IV would hunt for as long as ten hours at a time; exhausting at least five horses and often coughing up blood in the process. Records have it that he also once hunted down a stag without the aid of hounds but sadly, fail to recount how he managed this particular triumph!

Since 1948, the park surrounding Chambord has been a national reserve for *le chasse* and covers some 13,600 acres; no wonder then, that, what with both modern and ancient sporting connections, the château was chosen, way back in 1981, to be the permanent venue for the annual French Game Fair.

Hounds outside the chateau at Chambord…(*courtesy of JMS Pictorials*)

…Chambord as seen today

Reach for the skies!

Sporting lodges (known by the French as *pavillons de chasse*) are often used as a lunchtime venue for the members of the local commune *chasseurs*. In parts of southern France though, and especially in areas where doves migrate, it has long been traditional practice to either net incoming birds or to shoot them from towers built into the trees. Occasionally, these towers and lodge accommodation are combined – a practice which can lead to some quite unusual-looking buildings!

A dove shooting lodge in the south-west of France (*courtesy of JMS Pictorials*)

Italy

In the hilly Tuscany region, the hunting lodge is where everyone congregates in the morning and from where everyone is given a location and shooting position for the day. At one hillside lodge – and it may be common practice throughout Tuscany – the Guns form a circle around the shoot captain who takes a cartridge and throws it in the air. It sounds a slightly dangerous occupation but, whoever it is pointing towards when it lands is then allocated a number. Eventually, all will have theirs and then the captain calls out the numbers in order to give the men their position in the surrounding countryside.

Once all are in position, a team of dog-men beat through the cover and send wild boar (*cinghiale*) towards the waiting Guns. At an agreed time, shooting stops for lunch and then the sport continues for much of the afternoon... until the captain calls everyone back to the lodge via walkie-talkies. Vehicles are sent off to pick up the shot boar which are brought back and, at the hunting lodge, a butcher waits with sharpened knives and a scrubbed down block on which he cuts up the beasts as soon as they are brought in (and after being skinned and eviscerated, of course!). Everybody, the dog-men, shooters and the butcher himself, take away with them a bag of jointed meat. One bag is, however, always put into the lodge's freezer because, in February, the Guns hold a celebratory lunch at the lodge and cook whatever has accumulated in the freezer.

Austria

'The chamois is cunning and places sentinels on guard, so the hunter must be still more cunning, and scent them out,' so said children's writer Hans Christian Andersen in his book *The Ice Maiden*. Chamois has long been a much sought after quarry in regions of Austria – in particular on the borders of the provinces of Salzburg and the Tyrol. Rough, tough and mountainous, the area is not known for its ability to provide an easy walk, a successful stalk and back down the hill in time for tea and so, for this reason, chalets were constructed long before the area was popular with winter skiers.

Gerlos, an Alpine hamlet, was the perfect location for one such lodge – which was frequented each season by the Waring family.

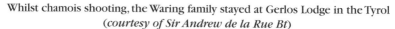

Whilst chamois shooting, the Waring family stayed at Gerlos Lodge in the Tyrol
(*courtesy of Sir Andrew de la Rue Bt*)

Antigua

If you were ever lucky enough to find yourself in the Eastern Caribbean…on the island of Antigua in fact, and fancied a bit of clay-shooting, one could do no better than visit Reservoir Range and shoot the lay-out designed by world champion clay shot Will Thatcher for the benefit of shooting ground owner and entrepreneur Geremy Thomas. Set in thirty acres, whilst the trap lay-out might be second to none, the shooting lodge is, with all its spectacular location and grandeur, also well worth a visit. Looking exactly like an upmarket African safari lodge, can there possibly be any better place to sit and enjoy your rum punch!

The quite spectacular lodge at Reservoir Range in the Caribbean
(*courtesy of Geremy Thomas/Antigua Clays*)

Africa

One cannot mention an African-style safari lodge as we have above without then including the real thing! There are plenty to choose from and they range from the most basic bush camp to luxuriously appointed permanent buildings set in the heart of scrub or, along the coast of East Africa, almost on the beach. Rustic or hotel-like, lodges catering for the game hunter or safari enthusiast can readily be found in Tanzania, Zambia, Botswana, Malawi, Namibia and Kenya.

It was in Kenya, at Treetops Lodge, where, in 1952, in the words of game hunter and author Jim Corbett, 'For the first time in the history of the world, a young girl climbed into a tree one day a Princess and after having what she described as her most thrilling experience she climbed down from the tree next day a Queen...' These few seemingly bizarre words recorded in the Treetops Lodge visitor's book were, of course, referring to the fact that it was here where Princess Elizabeth was staying the night her father, King George VI, died and she had, with immediate effect, become Queen Elizabeth II. Built in 1930, Treetops was originally nothing more than a two roomed building which was then doubled in size specifically for the Princess's visit. Two years later it was burned down by the Mau-Mau and eventually reconstructed in a much larger form in 1957. Recently further improved and the original 1957 parts renovated, it is nowadays owned by Aberdare Safari Hotels.

Interesting rustic lodges catering for the game shooter or safari enthusiast can be found in many places throughout Africa (the door in the Baobab tree is, believe it or not, the entrance to the men's toilet!)
(courtesy of Mandy Shepherd)

JOURNEYING TO THE LODGE

AFTER THE NORMAN CONQUEST when hunting with hounds first became a popular pastime with royalty and noblemen as a result of customs brought from France, travelling from a main residence to a hunting lodge many miles away involved a huge entourage. Similarly, when hawking was fashionable at the time of Elizabeth I, it must have been a logistical nightmare to ensure that dogs, hawks and all the necessary household equipment was transported safely by means of bullock wagons and horse and cart, the responsibility for which was all down to the Marshal – an officer in charge of all the household's horses, carts and wagons and transportation of goods. The gentry themselves rode on horseback to the lodge accompanied by grooms, squires and high-ranking household officials.

Medieval field sports frequently involved several days journeying to the lodge…often with a retinue of family retainers

'Secret houses'

During such times that the household were away hunting, lower members of staff remained at the main residence in order to carry out what might best be described as 'spring cleaning' – and when one considers the likely living conditions in even the grandest places, it was probably a very necessary operation! In later years whenever this task needed to be undertaken, the house owner and his family might well have de-camped to a secondary residence nearby. Such temporary (but nonetheless, equally as grand) homes were not, as was once thought, sporting lodges – there would have been little point when built so close to home – and have since gained the title of 'secret houses' or summer houses. One superb example of a secret house (although unfinished due to the landowner, Sir Thomas Tresham's death in 1604) can still be seen at Aldwinkle St Peter, Northamptonshire.

Sporting tourists began to visit the Highlands of Scotland during the late eighteenth century in order to shoot grouse and fish for salmon, travelling north on horseback or by stage coach (a journey which might take up to a week from London and cost in excess of £15), stopping off at coaching inns en-route and lodging at small country inns or with farmers and crofters once they had reached their moor or river – usually the property of a friend or acquaintance and made available to them free of charge.

During the first half of the nineteenth century when the fashion for owning or renting shooting and fishing in remote places was first becoming extremely popular, intrepid sportsmen still thought nothing of spending several days travelling to a shooting lodge in a far flung outpost of the Highlands of Scotland, the west of Ireland, Wales or the north-east of England. Initially making their journey on horseback, by horse drawn carriage or by steam ship (or a combination of all three), the rapid expansion of the railway system during the Victorian period simplified travel arrangements and enabled sportsmen to reach a destination virtually anywhere in the British Isles within the space of twenty-four hours.

The construction of the railways meant that journeys north were far more viable
(*courtesy of JMS Pictorials*)

In the late 1800s, those who lived in London and yet wanted to ride to hounds were faced with two possible alternatives; one being to keep their horses in town and take them down by train on hunting mornings, the second meeting them at the covertside to where they'd been taken from livery. The 8th Duke of Beaufort writing in 1885, told his readers that 'convenient trains serve practically all of the packs within easy reach of London' and went on to give a list of the most useful stations from which to depart and alight.

The motor car, which became popular with sportsmen who wished to hunt, shoot or fish during the Edwardian era, reduced journey times even further and short haul internal air flights, introduced during the mid-twentieth century, together with the gradual increase in the use of private charter helicopters in recent years, have all made it possible for modern day sportsmen to fly from the south of England to an isolated lodge in the Highlands of Scotland, the Outer Hebrides or Ireland in less than four hours.

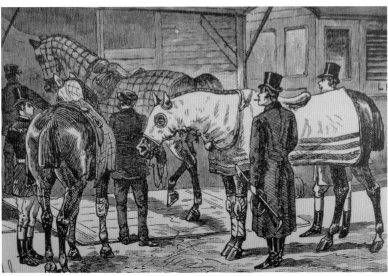

Hunters were occasionally loaded onto trains and transported from London to the provinces for a day's sport (*courtesy of JMS Pictorials*)

A NEW BREED

Realising that money could be made from shootings and fishings, a number of canny lairds started to let out the sporting rights on their property to wealthy English sportsmen, a practice which became increasingly common in the 1820s and '30s. In 1834, *Anderson's Guide to the Highlands and Islands of Scotland* observed that 'Moors may be had at all prices from £50 to £500 for the season, with accommodation varying according to the circumstances'. Seven years later in 1841, *The Inverness Courier* was more specific about rental values, stating that the going rate for ground capable of yielding 500 brace of grouse was £125 a month or if a good lodge was included, £250 (over £11,000 in today's prices).

The Highlands were now attracting a new breed of sportsmen, more often than not a fashionable aristocrat or a wealthy businessman, rather than country squire or former army officer who was quite happy to 'rough it' on his journey north. These men were not only prepared to pay relatively large sums of money for the privilege of shooting grouse, but also wanted to travel to their shootings and fishings in comfort. Many took a steam ship from London to Inverness, a journey which often took six or seven days to accomplish, then continued the journey to their shooting lodge by carriage.

The logistics of journeying to the lodge – and, of course, the quality of sport on offer – might well have dictated the likely cost of renting a lodge property. Rentals varied immensely, according to the size and quality of the lodge, accessibility by road and rail, the availability of a safe yacht anchorage if a coastal property and last but not least bag limits imposed by a landowner and his agent.

In 1901, a sporting tenant seeking a Scottish estate could expect to pay from £5,000 per annum (£285,300 in today's prices) for a top mainland deer forest, to around £120 (£7,000 today) for a large 20,000 acre mixed shooting in the Outer Hebrides. Grouse at this time were stated to be worth between £1. 10s. (£1.50) and £1. 15s. (£1.75) per brace; stags from £20 to £30 each and salmon from £2 to £10 per fish.

Clients invariably signed a rental or a lease agreement prior to taking a property, agreeing to pay staff salaries during the period of their tenure, reimburse the owner for any damage done to the lodge, to keep accurate records of game killed and to 'exercise the right of shooting and fishing in a gentlemanlike and sportsmanlike manner and to leave a sufficient stock of game for breeding'.

TRAVELLING IN STYLE

The owner or tenant of a shooting lodge and his family traditionally travelled from their town or country home to the lodge in time for the start of the sporting season, usually at the beginning of August if shooting grouse in Scotland, Ireland, Wales or northern England. As has been previously mentioned, he would more often than not, be accompanied by his butler, his valet, his cook, his wife's lady's maid, and his children's governess. In addition, if he owned a sporting estate elsewhere, his retinue might also include a gamekeeper to act as loader and also in the entourage might perhaps be included his favourite gun dogs.

Just how grand these arrangements might be can be seen from the travel plans of the Scott family (of which much more in *Life in the Lodge*). They arrived on North Harris in great style at the beginning of August every year, having travelled from their London home in Park Lane by train (in an especially reserved railway carriage), as far as Glasgow or Kyle of Lochalsh. The remainder of the journey was by sea across the Minch to their home, Amhuinnsuidhe Castle aboard their principal steam yacht, the 445 ton *Golden Eagle*. Their particular staff members included Sir Samuel's valet, a lady's maid and other key servants – together with Lady Sophie's kennel of prize winning Cairn terriers!

Sir Henry Peto and friends arrive at his Scottish sporting lodge in 1904

Arriving at the lodge in 1901

Geoffrey G. Braithwaite, then aged 11, recounts in his privately published autobiography, *Fine Feathers and Fish*, his family's arrival at Cat Lodge in 1901:

IN 1901, my father (Cecil Braithwaite) decided to take a small lodge and grouse moor in Scotland, namely Cat Lodge in Inverness-shire situated on the road between Newtonmore and Loch Laggan. It was at Newtonmore (railway station) that I first stepped foot in Scotland and the whole family and staff had breakfast at the Mains Hotel after which some of us proceeded by wagonette with a pair of horses hired from MacRae & Dick of Inverness, a pony and trap and with a farm waggon for the luggage. My brother and I together with a tutor set off riding our bicycles, the distance from Newtonmore to Cat Lodge being about twelve miles.

Cat Lodge was a very comfortable house but on the small side for the large family, so when we had two guests staying for the shooting, beds were arranged for them in cottages near at hand which we christened 'Kitten Cottages' and the ever faithful and trusted family servant, Obed Turner, who although being our coachman, assumed the duties of valet and general factotum during our stay, the horses being in the care of MacRae & Dick's driver.

An extract from the Inverness Courier, *7th August 1903*
Garve Notes

The shooting lodges in this district are rapidly filling up, and during the last few days Garve station has been very busy. On one day Mrs MacKenzie, of the Hotel, had about 30 horses waiting the arrival of the mail train to convey sportsmen and their luggage to the different lodges. Mr Walter Parrott, the genial tenant of Braemore, arrived on Saturday. On Monday he went out stalking, and grassed a fine royal and nine pointer right and left, both clean and in fine condition. Mr R. Lucas Tooth and party arrived at Strathgarve on Monday afternoon. He grassed a stag, fallow buck and roe buck in fine condition, the same evening. Mr Tooth very kindly presented the venison to several people in the village, and his generosity was much appreciated. Mr Fred Davis arrived at Inchbae, where sport promises well. Mr Paul d'Rubens of London, who has been ordered to Scotland by his medical advisers, has come to Corriemiollie Lodge and part of the shootings. The remainder has been let to Mr Maclaughan, who is to stay at the Garve Hotel. General regret is expressed that owing to bad health Mr Williams is unable to come to Strathvaich at present, but it is hoped that he may be able to come north in September fit and well. If the forest is not shot over many people, rich and poor alike, will miss Mr Williams' haunch of venison, as he was always most generous.

THE RAILWAY REVOLUTION

Inevitably, the dawn of the railway age in the Highlands made grouse shooting even more attractive to sportsmen, who could now travel north in a fast and comfortable overnight train from King's Cross or Euston. The railway reached Inverness in 1858, via a somewhat circuitous route from Aberdeen (this was followed by the opening of a more direct link via Perth in September 1863). By 1881, it was possible to leave London at 8pm in the evening and arrive at Perth by 8am the following day – and to be at Inverness at 1.30pm in time for a late lunch. The long winded journey to a shooting lodge by steamer, or by stagecoach with a wickerwork box fixed to the back containing pointers and setters had, almost overnight, become a thing of the past!

By the Edwardian era, rail services to Scotland were amongst the best in the country. Trains running between major stations not only offered fine dining facilities and sleeping accommodation, but conveyed a secure baggage van and 'dog kennel' compartments during the sporting season. Most sportsmen reserved a couple of first-class compartments for their party and a third-class compartment for their servants when travelling north for the shooting season.

The Midland Railway out of St Pancras ran a sleeper car service to Scotland via the spine of England to Carlisle and thence via Ayrshire. It is generally

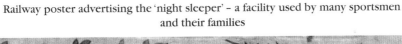

Railway poster advertising the 'night sleeper' – a facility used by many sportsmen and their families

thought that they were the first railway company in this country to offer a sleeping car service.

For those travelling to lodges or sporting hotels elsewhere in Britain, the journey was usually relatively simple – but did, however, sometimes involve an express train to the nearest principal station, a local train to a rural station or halt and onward transport by carriage or car to the final destination. Although undoubtedly tedious at times, these journeys could, in most cases, be easily accomplished from London within a day.

The boat-train

Sportsmen bound for Ireland in days gone by were able to take the boat-train from Euston to Holyhead, or from Paddington to Fishguard, from where they could catch a connecting train at their port of arrival, travel by onward express from the nearest principal station to their final destination station and then continue their journey by carriage or jaunting car to their shooting lodge or hotel. Somewhat surprisingly, it was usually less time-consuming to travel from London to far flung parts of the Irish countryside than it was to reach remote corners of the Scottish Highlands and Islands.

During the early decades of the twentieth century, it was possible to leave Euston at 8.45pm by the London & North Western Railway Irish Mail service, reach Dublin at 6.00am the next morning, depart from Broadstone Station at Dublin by the 7.00am Midland Great Western Limited Mail Service bound for Westport in Co. Mayo – the principal station for many of the Mayo lodges – and arrive at 11.45am, giving sportsmen the opportunity of afternoon or evening fishing. For those travelling to the south-west counties of Ireland, on the Paddington to Rosslare overnight service via Fishguard, a special connecting express to Waterford and Cork enabled anglers to be out on the Blackwater river by 10.00am the next morning!

The rail-sea-rail boat-train service continued to be the principal method of travel to Irish lodges and sporting hotels until the 1950s when sportsmen began to take cars by steamer to Ireland, or fly to regional airports and hire a car for the duration of their visit. Modern day sporting visitors to the 'Emerald Isle' either use one of the regular roll on-roll off car ferry services, fly-drive packages, or travel to their destination by helicopter.

Train hire and 'specials'

In the heyday of rail travel, many railway companies offered their customers a train-hire service. The 6th Duke of Portland annually chartered a 'special' to take him and his entourage from Welbeck Abbey (his Nottinghamshire seat), to Langwell, his sporting estate in Caithness, travelling the final leg of the journey in a motor car at the head of a procession of cars, carriages and carts. Sir Berkeley Sheffield, Bt, could not afford a complete train but, nevertheless, hired a private coach with sleeping accommodation: this was attached to a series of scheduled trains between Doncaster and Morar on the West Highland Line and enabled him and his party to travel in comfort between Normanby Park, his Lincolnshire home, and Meoble Lodge, his Highland deer stalking quarters – in this case the last stage of the journey, some twelve miles, was made by motor launch across Loch Morar.

Members of the Royal family traditionally used the Royal Train when travelling to Balmoral for the shooting season, arriving at Ballater station (which closed in 1966 and had a special royal waiting room), before making an onward journey by road. They also used the train, or chartered carriages on ordinary trains, when visiting various prestigious Scottish sporting properties as invited guests.

'The Flying Scotsman'

Referred to by many sporting enthusiasts as their favourite mode of transport for journeying north, there is often confusion regarding the name 'Flying Scotsman'. In actuality, it seems that the engine was one entity and the train another. As railway expert Michael Morant explained: 'The train's title is simply a catchphrase and a very good one it is, too.' Typical of the period 1925 to 1935 is the engine shown here, the Gresley A1 pacific No. 2563. According to Michael (and he out of anyone, should know!), at the time of the photograph 'the locomotive, was based at Edinburgh's Haymarket shed' and it was only used 'as motive power for the Flying Scotsman in the years 1929, 1930 and 1932.' Pictured here on its northbound journey, the photo was, so Michael believes, 'taken at … Woolmer Green between Welwyn and Knebworth... also of interest… is the vehicle behind the engine which is the much needed baggage van. All the carriages are teak bodied.'

'The Flying Scotsman' en route north (*courtesy of the Mike Morant Collection*)

Railway timetables and sporting guides

The ever increasing demand for Scottish shooting lodges and sporting estates during the late 1860s (further fuelled by the rapidly expanding railway network north of the border), prompted J. Watson-Lyall, enterprising editor/proprietor of *The Perthshire Constitutional*, a local newspaper based in Perth, to produce his first definitive travel guide for sporting visitors to Scotland in 1873. Realising that taking a Highland grouse moor, deer forest or salmon river with suitable lodge accommodation was an extremely complex business involving weeks of forward planning, he researched and published the less than snappily named

Sportsman's and Tourist's Guide to the Timetables, Rivers, Lochs, Moors and Deer Forests of Scotland in order to make life easier for visiting sportsmen. As the title suggests, this book was not just confined to the Highlands – the traditional destination for those in pursuit of grouse, salmon and stags – but covered every part of Scotland from the Border counties to the Orkney and Shetland Islands.

The Sportsman's Guide, as the publication soon became known, rapidly became an indispensable work of reference for all potential sporting tenants and contained lists of landowners, factors and tenants of virtually every grouse moor, deer forest, salmon river and shooting lodge, together with the acreage, annual rental and best road, rail or steamer route. Mr Watson-Lyall paid particular attention to the needs of anglers – providing detailed information about river lengths, loch sizes, hotels with fishing attached, river seasons, best months to fish, expected catches and the most suitable flies to use. By the late 1870s, the *Guide* had become so popular that it was being produced on a monthly basis at the price of one shilling (5p) per copy, the cost of publication being covered by advertisements from ' blue chip ' companies such as Cadbury's and Standard Life.

Cover of 'The Sportsman's Guide' – the inside pages of which were invaluable to anyone seeking information connected with fishing, stalking and shooting

Other providers of vital information

Mr Watson-Lyall was not alone in his endeavours to make life easier for any sportsmen travelling to a remote Scottish shooting lodge. In 1881, Robert Hall, proprietor of 'The Highland Sportsman Shooting and Estate Agency' based in Old Bond Street, London, produced an extremely high quality but sadly short-lived annual *Compendious Sporting Guide To The Highlands of Scotland*, complete with a set of fold-out maps; which not only featured all of the main sporting properties, the nearest railway station, post office and telegraph office, but also gave a brief description of each lodge and an estimate of the expected annual game bag. Several other agents followed suit, but none was able to surpass the success of *The Sportsman's Guide* which continued to be published at regular intervals until 1915 when it was finally disbanded in the wake of the outbreak of the Great War.

Elsewhere in the British Isles, sportsmen were not so individually well catered for, and had to rely on *Bradshaw's Railway Guide* or timetables issued by railway companies and steam ship operators in order to sort out the most suitable travel route to their shooting lodge, be it in Derbyshire, Devon, Wales or Ireland. If fortunate enough, they might also be provided with travel instructions by their landlord or, if fishermen, could perhaps refer to *Where to Fish*, a useful publication produced annually by *The Field* magazine, or to *How and Where to Fish in Ireland*, or similar works of reference containing train, steamer and accommodation information.

Changing times

Rail continued to be the preferred mode of travel for sportsmen visiting Scotland up until the outbreak of the Second World War in 1939 – although by this time it was not uncommon to send a chauffeur-driven car in advance, carrying guns, rods and other sporting impedimenta and food supplies. Some sportsmen even sent their wife along to accompany the chauffeur and to organise the domestic side of things in the lodge prior to their arrival, while they, themselves travelled north in comfort aboard the night sleeper train!

> In the build-up to the start of the 1936 grouse shooting season, according to the *Inverness Courier*, a total of eight trains conveying sportsmen and their parties 'arrived in Inverness from London between the hours of 8.30am and 11am' on Saturday 1st August; this was 'excluding the ordinary mail train' and 'a special train of motor cars belonging to shooting tenants resident in Inverness-shire.'

Following the cessation of World War hostilities in 1945, an ever increasing number of sportsmen chose to travel north to their lodge or hotel by motor car rather than by rail, or, in some cases, opted to fly from London to Aberdeen, Inverness, Stornoway and other Scottish regional airports, travelling by hire-car or taxi for the final leg of the journey. Those who continued to use the rail network were affected by service cuts made in the wake of nationalisation in 1948 and the closure of many rural lines after the 'Beeching Axe' of 1963.

Nevertheless, a few of the more traditional sporting types who prefer to travel north to their Scottish shooting or fishing quarters in style and comfort still use the Scotrail Caledonian Sleeper service, affectionately dubbed 'The Deerstalker Express'.

The Deerstalker Express

Departing from Euston station each evening, the 'Deerstalker Express' continues to make the nostalgic journey to destinations as far afield as Corrour, Rannoch, Fort William, Gleneagles or Inverness. In July 2002, co-author David S.D. Jones realised a long held ambition to travel to the Highlands overnight aboard the 'Express' – as a result of which are included his personal notes and observations as under:

SOME MONTHS PREVIOUSLY I had read the diaries of the Honourable Rupert Leigh who visited the Aline estate on the island of Lewis on a regular basis between 1910 and 1914 to shoot and fish with his brother, Lord Leigh, the sporting tenant. As I visit Lewis three or four times a year, it seemed a worthwhile project to follow in the footsteps of Mr Leigh from London to Aline, travelling by the Scotrail Caledonian Sleeper, ship, and road, noting some of the changes that have taken place over the past 90 years or so.

In 1913, Mr Leigh began his journey to Aline and, after an early dinner, he travelled by cab from his London home in Knightsbridge, to Kings Cross Station in time to board the 7.55pm Great Northern Railway night sleeper to Fort William. He arrived at Fort William at 9.50am the following morning, having taken a breakfast basket at Crianlarich. He then took a local train along the West Highland line to Mallaig, where he boarded the MacBrayne steamer S.S. *Sheila* bound for Stornoway on the Isle of Lewis. After a somewhat rough crossing, the ship docked (an hour late!) in Stornoway at 9.15pm. Mr Leigh spent the night at the Royal Hotel, departing for Aline after breakfast by chauffeur driven car and arriving at the lodge in time for Saturday luncheon at 1.00pm. Having swiftly fortified the 'inner man', he immediately went out on the Aline moors and bagged a brace of grouse in time for dinner!

My own journey to Aline began on the 18.45 service from Southampton to Waterloo in July 2002. After crossing London by tube from Waterloo, I arrived at Euston Station in time to catch the 21.05 train to Inverness, affectionately dubbed the 'Deerstalker Express.' It soon became apparent that I was about to embark upon one of the great rail journeys of Britain. After being greeted by an immaculately dressed Scotrail steward, who took my order for the complimentary breakfast, I was shown to a spotless cabin in the Inverness portion of the train – beyond Preston the train divides into three sections, with carriages for Inverness, Fort William, and Aberdeen. A trip to the luxurious first class lounge car for a Scottish 'night cap' was an obvious necessity, but upon entering, I was surprised at the variety of Scottish fare and beverages on offer – the food being served on real china plates with stainless steel cutlery. Chatting to a tweed clad gentleman, apparently a regular traveller, I was told that up until about thirty years ago many of the train stewards could advise on the best flies needed to fish particular waters, and could even give assistance tying them if required!

After a good night's sleep I awoke to the sight of red deer walking the hill somewhere near Aviemore. My train pulled into Inverness station shortly before 8.30am, the designated arrival time. Having spent the morning in Inverness, I took the afternoon Citylink coach to Ullapool in time to board the M.V. *Isle of Lewis* car ferry to Stornoway which departed at 17.30 and took approximately 2¾ hours to reach its destination. The ferry docked at 20.10. By 21.00 I had travelled the twenty-two miles to Aline by car over a good, if windy, road. My journey from London had been accomplished in just under twenty-four hours.

In 1913, Rupert Leigh was able to visit Aline as a guest of his brother, who paid an annual rental of £143 for the estate. Sadly, I could not afford to stay at the property, given that weekly hire rates in 2002 started at £3,500. I was a little too early for grouse shooting or stalking anyway, but during my fortnight on Lewis I did manage to hook a few brown trout on the nearby Barvas estate for the price of a £5 day ticket.

Rupert Leigh reached Mallaig by rail from London in approximately 14½ hours. My train journey from London to Inverness took about 12½ hours. His voyage to Stornoway was scheduled to take 8½ hours, whereas my combined coach and ferry journey was accomplished in five hours. I travelled from Stornoway to Aline by car in just over half an hour but it would have taken Mr Leigh in the region of three hours due to bad roads. Incredibly travel by public transport from London to Stornoway in 1913 took little longer than it does today.

Aline – the final destination!

Price wise, Rupert Leigh paid £8-16/-6d (£8.82½p) for his footman to travel to Lewis third class by rail and sea. He himself presumably travelled first class but I have been unable to ascertain what this would have cost. I paid a total of £137.30 for my return journey to Stornoway, the most expensive part being £99 for Apex rail travel on the Caledonian Sleeper between London and Inverness.

Travelling aboard the 'Deerstalker Express' en-route to the island of Lewis is a unique experience. I would urge any countryman to make the journey at least once, if only for the wonderful scenery and wildlife that can be observed from the carriage windows.

THE COMING OF THE CAR

Keen to take advantage of motor car freight traffic, rail operators began to put on special 'car trains' from London to various major Scottish stations during the shooting season in the 1920s and '30s, thus enabling sportsmen and their chauffeurs to travel north overnight in comfort, then collect their car upon arrival. These services later became a standard feature of rail travel to Scotland, eventually becoming British Rail Motorail, which conveyed cars belonging to members of the sporting fraternity until its demise in 1995.

In the very early years of the twentieth century, according to various contemporary accounts, sporting visitors to Scottish lodges regularly shipped motor cars by steamer from the General Steam Navigation Company Wharf on the Thames in London to Leith at Edinburgh, in the company of a chauffeur, who then drove the car on to the final destination. Cars bound for Outer Hebridean lodges in Lewis and Harris were then driven north to the Kyle of Lochalsh before being roped down to the deck of the mail steamer for onward transport to Stornoway.

Unsurprisingly, given the wealth of many shoot lodge owners, lessees and tenants, both past and present, they have often been amongst the first people to introduce the latest innovations in transport to many isolated parts of Britain. A report from the *Inverness Courier* dated 29th August 1899, had this to say on the subject: 'Stornoway – Mr Millar, the shooting tenant of Soval Lodge, has introduced to Lewis the motor car. On Monday several gentlemen were treated to a run on board, and all appeared delighted with their first trip in the motor car on the island. The roads, however, were not adapted to this kind of car, so that in the run to Soval it only covered a distance of nine miles in one hour and forty minutes.'

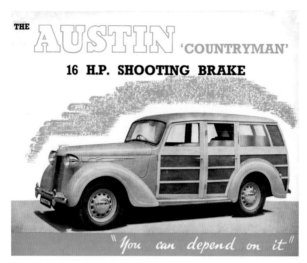

THE **AUSTIN** 'COUNTRYMAN'

16 H.P. SHOOTING BRAKE

"You can depend on it"

No true sportsman could afford to be without a motorised 'shooting brake' to get
him to and around his far-flung estate!

Driving all the way

As we have seen, some Edwardian sportsmen took advantage of the constantly
improving road system, sending a chauffeur-driven car north to their lodge by
road rather than by sea to await their arrival at the start of the season. Others
arranged for a car to be roped onto a flat-bed railway wagon and sent in stages
by a succession of mixed goods trains to Perth, Inverness or Aberdeen – the
chauffeur travelling by passenger train to the pick-up station.

However, from the 1920s onwards, it became increasingly common practice
for sportsmen, especially those of the younger generation, to drive to their
Scottish lodge alone, or with a chauffeur or valet for company (and to act as
relief driver), the rest of their party travelling north by train. By the late 1940s,
though, owners and tenants frequently drove north in their Rolls-Royce, Bentley,
Jaguar or other fast vehicle, with servants, dogs, guns and rods following behind
in a retinue of Land Rovers or jeeps.

The motor car also started to replace the train as the preferred mode of
transport to English and Welsh sporting destinations, with chauffeur-driven cars
and luxury shooting brakes being used. Some of the more enthusiastic shots of
the day, such as Brigadier Sir Joseph Laycock, who spent much of the season
travelling from shoot to shoot, actually slept in the back of their car at night
while their chauffeur or valet drove them on to their next shooting engagement!

Luxury saloon cars have since been replaced by the Range Rover, first
introduced in 1970, along with other versatile four wheel drive estate cars and

comfortable pick-ups, which can not only travel at high speed along motorways and major roads but can be used for transport on hill, moor and river bank.

Henry Grey Thornton and his Ford V8 shooting brake circa 1930 (*courtesy of the Thornton family*)

Henry Palethorpe, proprietor of Palethorpe's sausages and purveyor of the famous 'Royal Cambridge' sausage, lived in the Black Country and, during the first three decades of the twentieth century, regularly travelled up to his Anglesey shooting lodge, Ty Herion, by train from his country home near Kidderminster in Worcestershire. In order to have transport around his shoot throughout the season, Palethorpe was apparently in the habit of hiring local chauffeur-driven cars!

SHIPPING SERVICES

The enterprising Victorian and Edwardian engineers who developed the Scottish railway network ensured that many of the regional sea ports were served by railway lines, enabling sportsmen to cross the sea swiftly and comfortably by steamer to the various lodges, deer forests, shootings and fisheries in the Inner and the Outer Hebrides, and other islands situated off the West Coast, as well as in the Orkney and the Shetland islands. Many of the West Coast steamers were operated by David MacBrayne and Co. and ran in connection with scheduled train services, while those bound for the Orkneys and the Shetlands left Aberdeen for Stromness, Kirkwall or Lerwick – the journey to the latter port sometimes taking up to twenty-four hours through extremely rough seas.

Over the past half century or so, all of the principal steamer services have, like those that once plied their trade to Ireland, been replaced by modern roll-on-roll-off car ferries, which can convey commercial vehicles, cars and their passengers to the Hebridean and West Coast islands, the Orkneys and the Shetlands at vastly reduced journey times. These ferries are particularly popular with large sporting parties with rods, guns, dogs and other impedimenta, who can break their journey from the south in the bar-lounge for a few hours before driving on to their island lodge or hotel.

In bygone days, many of the more prestigious Scottish estate owners and lessees, particularly those with properties situated in isolated West Coast locations or on the Hebridean islands, owned a substantial private steam yacht which was used for travel from west coast ports and railheads such as Fort William, Mallaig and Kyle of Lochalsh to their shooting lodge – and to collect supplies of household provisions, coal and other essential commodities from the nearest coastal town on a regular basis. These yachts were also used to transport sportsmen from the lodge to remote stalking and shooting beats, easily more accessible by water than over land.

Throughout the 1840s, Inverness was, for a short period each year, overwhelmed by hordes of sportsmen on the way to their hired grouse moors. In August 1847, *The Inverness Courier* reported that:

'Preparations for the 12th August have been in full activity for some time; and during the last week sportsmen might have been seen hurrying to and thro, en-route to the quiet domains in the hills. From the east there were four steam ships arriving in Inverness in the course of three days, two from London and two from Leith – all freighted with the muniments of a grousing campaign. The steamers by the Caledonian Canal have almost daily

unloaded their freights; while every coach and car that rolled o'er stony streets brought full additions of welcome visitants to crowd for a time the Highland capital – thence bound for mountain and moor.'

VISIT ORKNEY AND SHETLAND

THE ANGLER'S PARADISE

★ Burn, Loch and Sea fishing at its best—where good baskets are the rule—not the exception.

★ In Orkney's numerous lochs (amongst others, Boardhouse, Swanney, Hundland, Stennes, Harray and Kirkbuster), good sport is assured.

★ In Shetland, within a six-mile radius of **St. Magnus Hotel**, are 17 lochs, innumerable voes and burns, where sea and brown trout of good size are plentiful.

THE NORTH OF Long hours of daylight—the fine bracing climate —the "different" atmosphere and outlook, make Orkney and Shetland the angler's paradise.

Write us for particulars, gladly sent post free.

SCOTLAND & ORKNEY & SHETLAND STEAM NAVIGATION CO. LTD

Dept. B. 23, MATTHEWS' QUAY, ABERDEEN, or Dept. B. 23, TOWER PLACE, LEITH

1930s poster advertising the services of the North of Scotland & Orkney & Shetland Steam Navigation Co.

ON A WING AND A PRAYER!

Sportsmen began to use commercial air services to travel from England to Scotland, or from the Scottish mainland to the larger islands en-route to shooting lodges, in the 1930s. At this time it was not uncommon for a tiny plane to land in a grass field or on a beach to disembark or to take on board passengers. In fact, on the Isle of Harris in the Outer Hebrides, the proprietor of the Rodel Hotel, Jock Macallum, doubled as the agent for the airfield at Northton, as well as offering fishing and shooting to paying guests on the Rodel estate. The single fare for anglers flying from Inverness to mainland Shetland in 1938 – a 2¼ hour journey – amounted to £4.

Short-haul internal air services improved dramatically during the late 1940s and '50s, making air travel extremely attractive to a new generation of anglers and shots, who had little time to spare. Indeed, many wealthy sportsmen now fly from England and elsewhere to Scottish regional airports, prior to taking a private charter helicopter to the larger shooting lodges, some of which have purpose-built helipads.

Private planes and luxury travel

Executive jets have now replaced the earlier types of private plane and are regularly used by sportsmen travelling to Scottish estates, particularly those in the Highlands, the final leg of the journey being made from Inverness or Aberdeen airport to the lodge by helicopter, luxury car or four wheel drive vehicle.

Private aircraft first became popular during the 1950s and were used by sportsmen to travel to Scottish shooting lodges. Sir Thomas Sopwith, the pioneer aviator, who owned the Amhuinnsuidhe estate on the Isle of Harris from 1946 until 1961, not only flew from the south of England to the nearest airport at Stornoway aboard a private plane when visiting the property but, according to local tradition, sent his Bentley and chauffeur ahead aboard his own personal

For those without their own, there are several helicopter hire companies that can provide transportation from urban areas to the most remote of sporting lodges
(courtesy of PDG Helicopters Ltd)

Bristol Freighter transport plane. John Foster Robinson, another Outer Hebridean proprietor, who owned Morsgail Lodge on the Isle of Lewis from 1955 until 1978, regularly flew his fishing friends to Lewis aboard his private plane, the *Croxley*, which made the journey from Filton airport near Bristol to Stornoway within the space of two hours, while the guests sipped champagne and ate turkey sandwiches!

Cecil Braithwaite, a retired London stockbroker and enthusiastic angler, then aged eighty-two years, recounts his first flight from Stornoway on the Isle of Lewis to Inverness in 1944 at the end of a sojourn at Grimersta Lodge in his privately published memoirs, *Happy Days with Rod, Gun and Bat*: 'My son (Geoffrey) arranged for us to fly back from Stornoway to Inverness, which took us fifty minutes. Had we gone by boat and train it would have taken us at least ten hours, with the discomfort of leaving Stornoway at the hour of 3am and the crowded train from Kyle of Lochalsh to Inverness. It was the first time that I had flown, and I enjoyed it very much in a most comfortable aircraft.'

TRAVELLERS FROM ABROAD

Sportsmen from overseas have been visiting Scottish shooting lodges and estates ever since the late Victorian period, either as tenants or guests. Wealthy Americans crossed the Atlantic by luxury liner to Southampton or Liverpool then travelled north by train to shoot grouse and to stalk deer. Prior to the outbreak of the First World War, German and Russian princes and nobility regularly sailed across the Channel in pursuit of the grouse, salmon and stags readily available on aristocratic sporting properties.

During the early years of the twentieth century, many Indian Maharajahs and princes made the long sea journey from India to England in order to indulge in their love of field sports. Among them was the Rajah of Kashmir, who rented Douglas Castle and shootings in Lanarkshire from the Earl of Home for the 1912 season, Maharaja Holkar of Indore, who visited Alladale in Ross-shire to stalk deer in 1913, and H.H. Prince Nazir Ali Khan, who spent several weeks at Grimersta Lodge on the Isle of Lewis in 1909 fishing for salmon and sea trout.

Scottish lodges continue to attract overseas visitors today, particularly American businessmen and wealthy Europeans with an interest in deer stalking and grouse shooting, who, unlike their early predecessors, can usually only afford to stay for a week or two at a time rather than for the whole season as was once the case!

LIFE IN THE LODGE

❦

GENERATIONS AGO, our wealthy sporting forbears took things at a leisurely pace, frequently spending the entire season living in their own or a hired lodge, fishing, shooting or stalking to their hearts' content. The more dedicated Scottish lodge habitués often arrived in late spring for salmon fishing, turned their attentions to stag and grouse from August onwards, then remained in the north until late October or early November to shoot woodcock. Some even took a break at the beginning of September, travelling to Yorkshire or East Anglia for a fortnight's grouse or partridge shooting!

George Malcolm, writing in *Grouse and Grouse Moors* in 1910, has this to say regarding the likely requirements expected by those who rented a lodge for the season:

> YOUR FIRST-CLASS SPORTING TENANT – English or American; never Scottish and Irish, and seldom any of the Continental peoples – gives liberally for his privileges, and exacts liberal advantages besides the bare right to shoot. The lodge must be commodious – furnished and kept almost up to the standard of metropolitan modern life. Electric lighting, garage for motor cars, facilities for yachting and salmon fishing where practicable, and many other luxuries, or, as some would say, superfluities, are now looked upon as indispensable; while every department of the internal economy of the house, especially the culinary arrangements, must be in quite first-rate order and capacity.

Today, few sportsmen can afford to rent a shooting lodge and the associated shooting, fishing or deer forest for more than two or three weeks annually. Those lucky enough to actually own a lodge invariably live elsewhere on the estate and let the lodge for as many weeks as possible in order to make the property pay its way. Indeed, some landowners claim that sporting lets generate insufficient income, forcing them to subsidise the running costs of their lodge and estate out of their own pocket!

HOW LODGE LIFE WAS

In the heyday of the sporting lodge, lengthy preparations were required before arrival, particularly if it was a rented property. Food, wines and spirits needed to be ordered from a reputable supplier; temporary servants engaged and travel arrangements considered. Further, it was considered courteous for a tenant to send letters of introduction to the housekeeper and the head gamekeeper.

Provisions and gifts

Two or three days before he was due to arrive at Ty Herion, his shooting lodge on West Anglesey, Henry Palethorpe would arrange for large crates of hams and other meats, huge pork pies with eggs in the centre, sausages, polony, kegs of beer, bottles of spirits and tins of cigarettes to be sent up from the Palethorpe factory at Tipton to provide sustenance for his guests, his staff and the beaters. At Christmastime, he would send another consignment of similar fare up to the lodge for distribution amongst the tenant farmers and others associated with his shoot – a gesture which, as one might imagine, was much appreciated in the locality!

Staff and personnel

Welsh shooting lodges were usually relatively small and required fewer staff, both inside and outdoors - even if a large shooting estate was attached. Lodges in Wales were traditionally occupied by the owner or his friends rather than let out on an annual basis. The sporting season was much shorter, too, with the owner spending two or three weeks at his lodge for grouse shooting during August and early September if a grouse moor was attached, and making week-end or weekly visits for rough shooting or wildfowling during the autumn and winter months.

Elsewhere, however, large shooting lodge establishments, particularly those in the Highlands and Islands of Scotland were major employers, retaining a resident housekeeper, one or two gardeners to maintain the surrounding grounds, a groom, a 'grieve' (farm foreman), a couple of men to look after the home farm (which supplied milk, eggs, beef, mutton and other produce during the sporting season), and either a full or part-time 'factor' (estate manager) to oversee every aspect of estate living. Gamekeepers, stalkers and ghillies would be employed, too, as well as part-time 'river watchers' if the property contained a fishery. The permanent staff would be augmented by locally recruited maids and part-time ghillies when the owner or tenant was in residence.

As a typical example of just how many people might be employed as a result of a sporting lodge being in existence, it is interesting to note the situation at the 62,000 acre Amhuinnsuidhe and North Harris estate during the Edwardian era. Owned by Sir Samuel Scott, a member of the Scott banking dynasty, the estate occupied the whole of the northern portion of the Isle of Harris in the Outer Hebrides and employed a permanent staff of around thirty people whose combined duties were to look after the main house, estate and the subsidiary shooting lodge, Ardvourlie Castle. These included six stalker/keepers under the command of headkeeper, Ewen Macdonald, and a blacksmith to shoe the 'garrons' (stalking ponies) – as well as carry out minor engineering work. In addition, Sir Samuel engaged a large number of part-time ghillies, river watchers, pony-men, maids and cleaners to help out during the sporting season. Everyone on his payroll received free salmon and venison as part of their emoluments and was invited to the annual Ghillies' Ball which he held at Amhuinnsuidhe Castle before he and his wife, Lady Sophie, departed for England at the end of the season each year (of which more in *Customs, Traditions and Curiosities*).

Outdoor staff at Eishken Lodge circa 1900 (*courtesy of Pairc Historical Society*)

Transporting supplies

As well as providing home produced venison, salmon and lamb, those responsible for the smooth running of any lodge needed to bring in vast quantities of food, wines, spirits and other supplies for family, guests and servants. At Amhuinnsuidhe (situated as it was across the water), the S.S. *Dunara Castle*, was chartered to convey goods from Glasgow to the castle immediately prior to each season. The Scotts (owners at the time) also hired the Scalpay-based puffer, *Maggie Love*, to go back and forth to Troon in Ayrshire on a regular basis in order to collect the consignments of coal needed to heat both the main house and the shooting lodge. In addition, their own small steam yacht, the *Rover*, crossed from Amhuinnsuidhe Castle to Tarbert, the principal township on Harris, virtually every day to collect any guests or supplies that had arrived by public passenger steamer.

RULES OF THE LODGE

During the season, when the lodge was obviously likely to be full of guests, any time off was minimal – and in any case, being generally situated miles from anywhere, it was impossible for staff to be able to travel into town or do much more than go for a walk or sit quietly and read. In some lodges, there were rules regarding staff having visitors – but again, the isolated nature of most places meant that would be highly unlikely and so friendships (and liaisons!) were restricted to fellow employees.

Serious relationships were sometimes frowned upon by employers – to the extent that dismissal might be threatened. Nevertheless, it was quite common for female indoor domestic staff to be courted by those employed outdoors as gardeners, farm hands, gamekeepers and ghillies. Many would eventually marry and, rather than continue as a 'domestic' in the lodge, most became housewives caring for their husband and subsequent children.

At the grandest lodges, where important society guests were frequent visitors, domestic staff would have been expected to adhere to the same rules and standards as seen in the finest London houses. These might have included any or all of the following, which are based on *The Servant's Practical Guide* 1880:

• When being addressed, a servant should stand still and always look at the person talking.

- Never speak without being spoken to (unless to deliver a message or to ask a necessary question) – and if a question or statement from an employer or guest requires an answer, it should be given in as few words as possible.

- Likewise, when in the locality of one's employer and/or their guests, a servant should never speak to 'another servant or person of your own rank, or to a child, unless only for necessity, and then as little as possible and as quietly as possible'.

- Any orders should be acknowledged by a response – which should be suffixed by whatever form of address is appropriate, i.e.; 'My Lord', 'Sir', 'Ma'am', 'Miss'.

- Always 'give room': that is, if you encounter one of your betters, make yourself as invisible as possible and avert your eyes. If required to walk with a lady or gentleman in order to carry packages, or for any other reason, always keep a few paces back.

- No member of indoor staff is to receive any relative, visitor or friend into the house, without the prior consent of the butler or housekeeper. Any member of the female staff who is found to be fraternising shall be immediately dismissed.

- Expect that any breakages or damages in the house shall be deducted from your wages.

'In all households (during Edwardian times)…a kitchen-maid might have to be down by 4.30am. Cook herself was expected to be down not later than 6.45, and to find the housemaids busy on the hall, the stair-cases and reception rooms. If, as sometimes happened, the back stairs did not mount to the maid's quarters but stopped halfway up the house, there was a certain amount of dark and early tiptoeing past the bedrooms of the gentry.

Establishments varied, of course, in size and splendour, and it might happen that hardly had the guest…begun to feel his soul seeping back from its nocturnal ebbing, than a knock (on the bedroom door) introduced a footman with a folded suit over his arm and a pair of shoes, or rather boots, in his hand. His brief weather report was a prelude to discussion of apparel suited to the temperature and type of sport to be enjoyed.' Arnold Palmer: *Movable Feasts*; as quoted by Macdonald Hastings in his *'Country Book – a personal anthology'*

There were also specific rules for men servants and outdoor staff. At Eishken Lodge, circa 1900, the ones below were drawn up by Joseph Platt and enforced by either the butler or the head gamekeeper, whichever was most appropriate.

- No servant to shoot off any gun or rifle, except those who are authorised.

- No smoking allowed inside any house, room, or building, except in places arranged for.

- No keeper or servant to load cartridges or use gunpowder while smoking.

- No servant under any pretence, except the indoor servants, to sit or stay in the pantry, or interfere with the work of indoor servants.

- The butler or footmen will put the flasks in the inside gun room for the sportsmen in the morning, and the keepers and ghillies will get them there.

- All guns and rifles to be cleaned by the keepers (not by the ghillies), the same night they are used, and under no circumstances are they to be left dirty till next morning.

- The keepers will be responsible for all visitors' guns and sporting tackle, unless they have personal servants to look after them.

- Any servant not obeying these Rules; will have to take the consequences of their neglect.

- Anything going wrong in any department; must be reported at once, and the matter put right if possible.

- Any servant ordering anything without permission will have to pay for the articles himself.

- Every servant must conform to these Rules, or give notice at once.

Some lodge owners were more liberal with their staff than others – as this photograph illustrates. Taken in the early 1960s, it shows Captain and Mrs Perrins (of Lea & Perrins Worcester Sauce fame), owners of the Garynahine estate on Lewis, enjoying drinks with their keepers and ghillies in the lounge at Garynahine Lodge.

Average earnings

As the nineteenth century turned into the twentieth, live-in servants, who had all their expenses (food, lodging, clothes etc) taken care of, earned as little as £10 a year: those who were not as well looked after in kind might well have been paid in the region of the following amounts:

Scullery Maid £13
Kitchen Maid £15
Housemaid £16

Parlour Maid £20
Cook £20
Lady's Maid £24
Cook/Housekeeper £35
Butler £45 to £52
Housekeeper £35 to £45

(Figures taken from Board of Trade findings of 1890)

VOICES FROM THE LODGE

To get a feel of exactly what life was like in and around some of the more remote sporting lodges throughout Scotland, Wales and Ireland (as we've seen, England has very little in the way of 'proper' dedicated lodge buildings), one can do no better than recount the experiences of those who lived there.

Life at a remote Scottish shooting lodge for the gamekeeping staff and their families, although much more comfortable than that of the neighbouring crofters and small farmers, was, nevertheless quite challenging when compared with modern day living conditions – as Elizabeth Macinnes (who died in 2006) recalled in an interview with co-author David S D Jones:

> I WAS BORN AT THE HOME OF MY MATERNAL GRANDPARENTS in the parish of South Snizort on the Isle of Skye in 1918, the youngest of seven children. My parents Robert Dempster and Mary McRaild were married at Kinloch Rannoch in Perthshire in 1900, my father being a gamekeeper on the Rannoch estate, then a large deer forest owned by Sir Robert Menzies.
>
> In 1911, Mrs Jessie Platt, proprietor of the 69,000 acre Eishken Deer Forest on the island of Lewis engaged my father as a deer stalker and gamekeeper at Valamos, a remote location in the forest, accessible only by boat or by a seven mile trek over the hills to the nearest road at Eishken Lodge. Our family then moved 'lock; stock and barrel' from Aulich Cottage, our home at Rannoch, to the stalker's house at Valamos. Because of our remote situation, Ross-shire County Council provided us with a teenage pupil teacher who lived in as part of the family and educated my brothers and sisters.
>
> Mrs Platt paid my father the princely sum of £75 a year, provided him with free accommodation, clothing, venison, a dog keep allowance and allowed him the right to cut peat for fuel. Mrs Platt was particularly generous to the stalkers and their families. Every Christmas she had one of the bullocks which she kept at Eishken killed and gave a joint of beef to each family, along with a plum pudding, ensuring that everyone had a good Christmas dinner. She also invited all of the stalkers' wives to a special tea at Eishken Lodge at the end of the stalking season and presented each woman with a length of cloth suitable for the manufacture of children's clothing.
>
> When the First World War was declared in 1914 my father enlisted in the Lovat Scouts, the famous keepers and deer stalkers regiment raised by Lord Lovat. Our family then left Valamos to live with my mother's

parents on the Isle of Skye for the duration of the war. Once the war was over and father had arrived home safely, our family returned from Skye and settled down once more in the stalker's house at Valamos. I was a mere baby at the time but my brothers and sisters were growing up fast. My eldest brother, John, born in 1903, emigrated to Australia in 1924, never to return, while my sister, Mary Ann, sadly died in January1927, aged just twenty years, while working away in private service in Greenock.

Later in 1927, my father, Robert Dempster, left Eishken and took a stalker's position with Sir George Bullough on the island of Rhum in the Inner Hebrides, an extremely private place where everything was geared to deer stalking and everyone worked on the estate. Our family then moved from Valamos to the estate village of Kinloch. We now had neighbours for the first time and easy access to essential amenities such as a school, a shop, and a regular steamer service to the mainland!

Robert Dempster, Elizabeth Macinnes' father, whilst serving in the Lovat Scouts during World War One (*courtesy of the Dempster family*)

However, two years later in 1929, we lost our new found freedom. After receiving countless letters from Mrs Platt imploring him to re-enter her service, my father gave in to her request and the family returned to Eishken. This time, we were posted to Kenmore, a former shepherd's house on the shores of Loch Seaforth, almost as isolated as Valamos, having no road link, but with a slightly easier sea journey to the nearest crofting township. Mrs Platt, by now, was in her early eighties but still went out stalking regularly and remained in total control of the Eishken estate. Indeed, your face 'had to fit' at Eishken at all times. If you did something that upset Mrs Platt or her senior staff members in any way, they would make things that uncomfortable for you that you would want to leave of your own free will, if not, they would find a reason for sacking you!

Occasionally, my father would accompany Mrs Platt on her visits to the homes of regular ghillies to check that all was well. She was not behind on handing out advice if she thought that things needed improving. I remember my father talking about the time that they called with Neil Macritchie, a ghillie who had fourteen children. Mrs Platt lined the children up, counted them with her stick, then turned to Macritchie and said 'Now then Macritchie, this has got to stop, no more children!'

I finished my education in the mid-1930s and moved from Eishken to Greenock to work in private service. It was a life of work, work and more work, even with the advantages of electricity, gas, running water and a regular tram service into Glasgow. Apart from a few short visits to my parents at Kenmore, I did not return home permanently to the island of Lewis until 1940. On the 4th June that year, I married Finlay Macinnes from Rhenigadale in North Harris, a gamekeeper, and we went to work as gamekeeper and cook-housekeeper for Sammy Newall at Hamnaway Lodge in Uig on the west side of Lewis, an isolated spot reached only by a long boat journey or by a five mile walk over rough moorland to the nearest road at Brenish.

My husband, Finlay, was responsible for looking after the Hamnaway river system, a little used fishery which might yield a daily catch of around six to eight salmon, the Hamnaway brown trout lochs, which often produced a daily basket of over 100 fish and some rented rough shootings in the vicinity of the lodge which produced small bags of walked-up grouse and snipe. His main duties involved vermin control, a small amount of poaching prevention and looking after the herd of cows which supplied milk for Hamnaway Lodge. I, myself, was in charge of Hamnaway Lodge, which was little more than an enlarged keeper's cottage with a newly installed solid fuel cooker, a toilet and bathroom, lighted by oil lamps. Two bedrooms were reserved for sportsmen, who usually travelled in by fishing boat from Uig in Lewis or Huishnish on the island of Harris. Supplies of flour, sugar, lamp oil and other essentials needed for the lodge were purchased in bulk and either brought in by boat or delivered by lorry to the nearest road end then carried over the moor manually!

Sammy Newall, our employer, was a plain man, proud of his Yorkshire ancestry,

The redoubtable Mrs Platt in her latter years – in the capable hand of her personal ghillie, John Macleod (*courtesy of K R Mackay*)

who always fished with a rod and line rather than a fly. He enjoyed the simple life and expected his guests, ranging from head gamekeepers to colonels, to do likewise. His favourite dish was 'tatty and herring' and he spent his evenings playing cards, usually inviting my husband to join in with him and his friends. When staying at Hamnaway alone, Sammy would always dine with my husband and myself then sit chatting with us well into the night.

We spent twelve happy years at Hamnaway Lodge before leaving in 1952 to look after my ageing parents, who were still living on the Eishken estate. Finlay, my husband, then took a job as a stalker on the estate at Seaforth Head, a small township connected by road to the main road to Stornoway. We stayed at Seaforth Head until my husband retired in 1973, when we moved to Balallan, where a number of my relatives lived.

The bare essentials

Inventory of items in the stalker's house at Valamos belonging to the Eishken estate during the occupancy of the Dempster family:

1 Dresser	1 Iron washstand
1 Meal chest	1 Bed and bedding
1 Bench	2 Pairs of steps
4 Chairs	1 Boat

In Ireland, life in the lodge was possibly a little more laid back than in other parts of the British Isles, with less conventional ' house rules ' and, more often than not, somewhat colourful servants who were inclined to turn up late, be impudent to sportsmen and imbibe to excess. Owners and guests were usually either Irish, who were used to the eccentricities of some of their fellow countrymen, or impecunious Englishmen who could not afford to buy or rent a Scottish or a Welsh property, and were thus obliged to make the best of what they found – and usually enjoyed the experience!

Helen Spellman, whose family were key employees at Fermoyle Lodge at Costello in Co.Galway during the first half of the twentieth century provides an insight into staff conditions at an Irish sporting lodge during the 1920s and '30s:

MY FATHER, JOHN SPELLMAN, was head gamekeeper to the then owner, Brigadier-General Kenneth Kincaid-Smith, a British army officer, who lived mainly in England and let out the shootings and fishings on the Fermoyle Lodge estate to wealthy paying guests. He looked after a

2,000 acre mixed shoot, mainly grouse, partridges, woodcock, snipe and plover, and the Fermoyle fishery, which included an eleven mile stretch of the river Cashla with eight large salmon and sea trout lakes, and several brown trout lakes. His staff at this time included one under-keeper, fourteen full-time river bailiffs and a number of game watchers based in strategic places on the property. Game birds were not reared at Fermoyle and pheasants were seldom if ever seen or shot. Father operated a strict vermin control regime, paying a cash bounty to any member of the public who shot a cormorant and took it to him. He regularly caught poachers despite the careful watching of the shoot, the rivers and the lakes by his staff.

Life at Fermoyle was not without incident. In 1919, father successfully hid Sean Broderick, Officer Commanding the 4th Battalion, Galway Brigade of the I.R.A., in the lodge while he was on the run from the British 'Black and Tans'. Despite being beaten up by the soldiers, when they searched the lodge looking for Broderick, he convinced them that he was not there and Broderick was able to continue on his journey to a 'safe house' in the mountains. As a precaution, father released his gun dogs in the grounds of Fermoyle Lodge after the Black and Tans had departed, just to see that no one had been left behind!

Father was well off in comparison with many of his neighbours. In 1930 he was paid 35 shillings a week (£1.75) and was provided with a free house, a free suit of clothes every other year, and a motor car plus free fuel when the car was used on estate business. He was allowed to cut turf for fuel and was entitled to all of the wild geese and rabbits shot at Fermoyle. He had the use of the lodge gardens to grow his own fruit and vegetables and some fields where he kept cows, calves, hens and ducks.

My mother, Hannah, who had started her working life as the cook at Kilbrack House in Co. Cork, was employed as the housekeeper at Fermoyle Lodge and received a small salary as well as a new costume annually. She cooked for the guests during the sporting season and acted as caretaker of the lodge during the winter months. She was assisted by local girls who came on a daily basis from the nearest village and carried out cleaning and other duties. Many of these girls later went to England to work as 'domestics' and were replaced by their younger sisters.

In addition to the gamekeeping and fishery staff and the girls who worked in the lodge, men were employed to look after the gardens and the grounds and to carry out general estate maintenance. A chauffer was employed, too, to drive the lodge car and my grandfather, Pat' Spellman, a retired head keeper, was retained as general caretaker of the estate. Fermoyle Lodge was probably the largest employer in the district at this time.

Adaptable staff

Henry Palethorpe, was a keen shot and either rented or owned outright, the sporting rights over a large area of land on West Anglesey which centred on the shallow valley of the river Crigyll, including a duck and snipe bog and three large lakes.

Most Welsh lodges were, relatively, much smaller than those found elsewhere in the British Isles and therefore had less staff to run them. At Ty Herion, the Palethorpe shooting lodge was run almost entirely by Mr and Mrs Burbage who carried out the housekeeping and cooking duties – and were also expected to help out with pheasant rearing assisting single-handed gamekeeper, Hugh Hughes.

NB: Mr Palethorpe later replaced Ty Heirion with a new castellated lodge, Surf Point, on the seashore at nearby Rhosneigr, which became known locally as 'Sausage Castle'! An all-round sportsman, he helped found the Anglesey Golf Club in 1914 and was a generous benefactor to various good causes in the area.

Henry Palethorpe, together with guests and staff members

SPORTING LIFE ON A DAILY BASIS

Before the First World War, it was not uncommon for sportsmen who stayed in the larger Scottish shooting lodges to go out on the hill, moor, river or loch in pursuit of grouse, salmon, stags and other game on every day of the week except the Sabbath. The same activities were rarely undertaken on consecutive days so a sportsman might spend a relaxing day angling for salmon and sea trout after an energetic day in the deer forest or on the grouse moor – particularly if the grouse were walked-up over a vast expanse of moorland.

Notes from a diplomat's journal

Sir Francis Denys, a member of the British Diplomatic Service, who kept a detailed journal of his lengthy annual shooting, fishing and stalking visits to a variety of lodges in Scottish Highlands and the Outer Hebrides from 1880 until 1905, provides us with some brief vignettes of sporting life during this period:

EISHKEN LODGE, ISLE OF LEWIS SEPTEMBER 21st 1883
I left the pony cart near Loch Erisort, and went to the bog which I found full of snipe. I blazed away half my cartridges for six snipe. Could not hit them, the birds twisting. Found few grouse on my beat and killed only 8½ brace of which 13 were old cocks. Ground very bare, with no covert.

UIG LODGE, ISLE OF LEWIS OCTOBER 12th 1886 – 9.30am–7.45pm
A wet morning, clearing at 9am. I started with Miss Murray and Miss Gage to try and find a shootable stag. We rowed up Loch Suainaval, and found the moor soaking wet with the previous night's rain. Nothing daunted the ladies started, walking up the glen, between the lochs, to the first hill, up which they went without a check, then across the valley to Cleite Fhidigidh where we lunched. Then up Teinnasaval where we came upon a young stag, a fresh one from Harris. By this time we were thirsting for blood and he was doomed. Leaving the ladies where they had a full view of the stalk, I walked round the hill to get to the leeward side of the deer, and after a short crawl, MacDonald (the stalker) got me within 60 yards, and I had a hurried and very close shot at him, as his shoulder was partly covered by the head of a baby stag, but luckily killed him dead at 4.45pm. The ladies then came up to see him. After the successful finish we made tracks for the boat, which we reached before dark, the ladies walking gallantly to the last, reaching the Lodge at

7.45pm. both very wet. Keepers and ghillies much surprised at the ladies pluck, MacDonald having confided to me in the morning his opinion 'that they would not get very far.' Wind S.W.

FOICH LODGE, ULLAPOOL, ROSS-SHIRE OCTOBER 2nd 1894

Had a day in Sir John Fowler's forest, Braemore with McHardy the head stalker as dry-nurse. We rode a regular cavalcade halfway up one of the numerous high hills. McHardy took up a position at the pass on Sheanadhchlair having previously sent a ghillie round to move up the deer towards us. The leading hind took the wrong direction and only a small yellow stag with some hinds came on sight. Firing at his chest I unfortunately hit him in the muscle of the left fore-leg and was not allowed to follow him. At 5pm. I was given a stalk and a downhill shot at a 'Royal' broadside on at 120 yards and shot over him – this on Dhearg – then rode home. With paths up every hill, which one can ride, certainly takes the glamour from the sport.

GRIMERSTA LODGE, ISLE OF LEWIS JULY 27th 1895

Fished all day in the upper stream of Number Three Loch. The shoals of salmon beggar description leaping in every direction and the shallow water alive with their back fins. I had a rise every 8 to 10 casts between

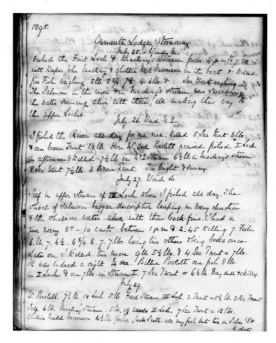

A page of Sir Francis Denys' journal from 1895

1 pm. and 2.45, killing seven fish, 6 lbs., 7 lbs., 6½ lbs., 6¾ lbs., 8 lbs., 7 lbs., 7 lbs., losing two others and being broke once. Later on I killed two more, 9 lbs., 5½ lbs., and four sea trout = 7 lbs. It was indeed a sight to see. Day dull and chilly. Wind N.E.

KILLILAN LODGE, STROME FERRY, ROSS-SHIRE September 16th 1903
Met Mr Bowerman [the owner, a London solicitor and property developer] at Kyle, had a lovely sail up Loch Alsh and arrived at Killilan for tea. Next day 8.30am drove 7 miles to Carnach walked up new path behind new hut, and took the direction of An Fitheach 2,874 ft, near the top we got rather lazy and shot at a young stag, but left him. Then spied two good stags on the grassy slope, stalked them, but they got our wind. Next tried a fine stag lying down not far from where I ate my lunch. Made a long circuit back but he also got our wind. Wending our way towards the Swan Loch homewards at 5.15pm. came across a young stag and some hinds. It being so late, I killed him. He turned out to be the same eight pointer I had left in the morning. Weight, 13 stone 10 lbs. clean. Ainsworth, stalker. Beautiful broken stalking ground, saw lots of deer. Wind S.E. Home 7pm.

In 1886, Sir Francis Denys (author of the journal quoted above), was moved to write a poem about life at Eishken Lodge. Jessie Platt, the owner's wife, was an early lady stalker and gave female guests priority over the men-folk when the day's sport was allocated – hence the sentiments contained within the poem!

The Sportsman's Lament – or A Day at Park, Lewis.

T'is not a lark to stay at Park where woman's rights prevail; to sit with Joe you'll only go, for sport to get you'll fail.
For Mrs Platt is very fat, and Mr Platt the same: Mr Platt at home he sat while madame killed the game.
The wretched guest, he beats his breast and smokes indoors his pipe; while far and wide does Jessie stride and shoots the grouse and snipe.
On Malcolm's back, just like a sack she's borne o'er hill and strath, then from a cragg she misses her stag and kills a hind and calf.
But should you wish to catch a fish, to Park you'd better hie: for n'er a shot by man's been got, when Mrs Platt was by.
In hope forlorn her guests have gone and swear its' all a do.
Though bidden thrice by letters nice, don't go if I were you.

SPORTING LIFE ON A REGULAR BASIS

Here Rhoderick Macleod describes sport at Scaliscro Lodge, on the Isle of Lewis during the late 1920s. Scaliscro had been purchased in 1926 by his father, Dr Norman Macleod, M.D., from the executors of the soap magnate, Viscount Leverhulme, for the sum of £1,000 and included a small lodge as well as a 10,000 acre estate with mixed shooting and fishing.

AS I REMEMBER in those years we caught very few salmon, nearly all on Loch Langavat and Loch an Fhir Mhaoil, Loch Airigh a Bhealaich and Loch an Easa Ghil (the latter being rented from the Grimersta estate) all of which were fed from the Grimersta river system. There was good sea trout fishing in Loch Suirstivat, particularly after we dynamited the falls on that river. Both Loch Ahalthair and Loch Tungavat on the Drovenish river provided good sea trout fishing also. We ran a small salmon and sea trout hatchery to restock these lochs. As to brown trout, you could take your choice of a score of lochs that held fish of 1lb and over. As a small boy of under 10 I used regularly to come home with over a dozen trout of ½lb or more. The stalking was poor because the main chance for a beast was as they moved from the Morsgail forest to Ben Mohal or Ben Mocacleit and the Drovenish high ground. Hinds were plentiful. As to shooting, we shot grouse over dogs (Gordon Setters) and could expect to have around 200 brace in a good season. You had to work hard for them as the birds sat very tight and a typical day on the Loch Langavat beat involved at least a fifteen mile walk. There was good snipe shooting near the lodge and the occasional woodcock was to be found. Duck were available, particularly on the north march at the entrance to Little Loch Roag.

LIVING THE DREAM

There were, of course, some sporting enthusiasts, wealthy and otherwise, who lived the 'lodge lifestyle' on a more or less permanent basis for many years. Usually of independent means, these men participated in field sports activities whenever the opportunity arose.

Henry Grey Thornton was one such man. He owned a number of lodges in England and Scotland and, throughout the late 1920s, 1930s and early 1940s, divided his time between his Exmoor sporting lodge at Morebath (Warmore House), his wooden fishing lodge in Argyll (situated near his private stretch of the river Awe), and Soval Lodge on the Isle of Lewis. The latter was at the hub of his 35,000 acre sporting estate – which boasted grouse moors, woodcock and wildfowl shooting and a first-rate salmon river. Henry spent the autumn and winter months hunting and shooting in Devon and Somerset. He went ferreting for rabbits in February and March and fishing for trout in the river Exe in April and May. In June, he fished for salmon in the river Awe, prior to travelling to Soval in July to fish for salmon, sea trout and char. He then spent the first week in August shooting wildfowl at Soval before returning home to Exmoor in time for the start of the autumn stag hunting and shooting seasons!

An expensive business!

Gilbert Holmes, another shooting lodge devotee, spent the greater part of his adult life (from the early 1920s until the mid 1950s) either renting or buying a succession of Scottish sporting properties, lived the 'lodge lifestyle' on a permanent basis – working his way through two huge inherited fortunes into the bargain. His tally of estates included the Glenfeshie, Ardlair, Inchbae and Kinlochewe deer forests and the 30,000 acre Gress estate on the Isle of Lewis, which he rented on two occasions.

Gilbert Holmes in the uniform of the Seaforth Highlanders during World War One
(courtesy of the Holmes family)

An old Harrovian and a keen piper, who had turned down a commission in the Guards in order to serve as a private soldier in the regimental pipe band of the Seaforth Highlanders during the First World War, Gilbert was an extremely popular man with rich and poor alike, and when he took Gress for the second time in 1945, he cured fish poaching activities by reaching an agreement with members of the local poaching fraternity, whereby they stopped netting the Gress river in return for the right to fish for salmon on the condition that they provided him with details of catch returns. Thereafter, he only prosecuted one poacher during the remainder of his tenure – a Dingwall naturalist who had shot two black-throated divers on the estate for his specimen collection!

Life at Glenquoich Lodge in 1850 – as described by an anonymous guest of the proprietor, the Right Honourable Edward Ellice, M.P., a London merchant involved with the Hudson's Bay Co. and the West Indies trade:

'We arrived at Glenquoich about 3 o'clock, anticipating dinner would be at six; but in order that the sportsmen might have as much light as possible the clocks of the establishment were put forward two hours, so that the breakfast hour was seven instead of nine, and the dinner hour four instead of six. We consequently had to make a hurried toilet.

The lodge was truly a shooting-lodge, furnished in the simplest manner with cane-bottomed chairs, and iron bed-steads. The bedrooms were small but numerous, and the whole system of living was simple and rational. Of course there were Highland cattle and mountain sheep, and such abundance of the sports of the river, the sea, and the field, the fare was undoubted and abundant. But the peculiarity of the entertainment was that immediately after dinner, a large tray of toddy tumblers was brought in by the butler, and placed with solemnity before Mrs Ellice, the charming wife of Mr Ellice, Jnr., who with practised art mixed up the grateful potation – our sole allowance.

Of course the gentlemen were early on the mountainside, while the ladies occupied themselves in boating, driving, walking, writing, sketching, and quiet gossip.'

DISTRACTIONS AND AMUSEMENTS

If, as it seems from the account of the guest of Edward Ellice, that the ladies 'occupied themselves in boating, driving, walking, writing, sketching, and quiet gossip' whilst the men-folk were out on the hill, there were other times when life in the lodge required some sort of further diversion and amusement.

To this end, such establishments often had an extensive library containing the latest sporting works and bound copies of periodicals such as *The Field*, as well as a substantial ballroom where dancing to the accompaniment of the resident piper or a specially hired orchestra took place in the evening once or twice a week.

Valley House, the shooting lodge on the inter-tidal island of Vallay off North Uist in the Outer Hebrides, was, in addition to it being a sporting venue, also used as a base for conducting antiquarian, archaeological and natural history fieldwork by the owner, Erskine Beveridge, a Dunfermline linen baron, and his sons, George and Fred, Edwardian sporting visitors could inspect historic artefacts, stuffed birds and rare works of art in the 'lodge museum' on the upper floor as a diversion from shooting and fishing!

Keeping children entertained (and clean!) might have proved difficult at isolated lodges without much other than sport in the way of a distraction

COOKING
AND CUISINE

❦

'CUISINE' might be too fine a word to use when it comes to cooking in the typical shooting lodge – it conjures up images of delicately prepared and beautifully served small portions; which is most probably not the case in the majority of places where hearty, wholesome food is required by sportsmen and women who are either expecting a hard day out in the open or have just returned from one! There are of course, exceptions and in some establishments, the dishes produced would not disgrace the reputation of several well-known top-class restaurants.

In the past, cooking facilities and the opportunity for a meal in shooting lodges were many and varied. At one end of the scale, the remotest and therefore most basic – generally used as an overnight refuge because whatever sport was being enjoyed was at a point too far away to return there and back in a day – might be equipped with nothing more than a fireplace and small iron range.

Even here, the sporting gent could well have had a 'Gentleman's gentleman' to accompany him during his isolated sojourn. Not only would this factotum carry all that was necessary to wherever it was needed; he might well be expected to act as loader, dog-handler and, quite literally, bottle-washer and cook.

In order to facilitate the latter, one or two of these remote lodges were equipped with stoves such as the one invented by Frenchman Alex Soyer which worked on similar principles as an oil lamp in that fuel was drawn to the burner via a wick. There are references to a gentleman's factotum using a Soyer Stove to cook meals in a remote bothy type lodge in the Outer Hebrides in 1851. On it he apparently produced a meal of 'eggs, mutton chops and fried sausages' (he also carried 'salt beef' as back-up!)

If the lodge accommodation really was (as they quite often were) nothing more than a simple stone-walled, corrugated or heather-thatched roofed affair built expressly for grouse shooting or fishing for trout out in the wildest of topography, it could well have been a part of the servant's duties to gather naturally occurring fuel in order to light a fire or stove – on which he was then expected to cook for his employer.

One could reasonably assume that, that after a successful day's sport in such places, there should at least have been the elements of a main course quite literally in the bag. Sadly this appears not always to have been the case: as J.E. Marriat-Ferguson pointed out in 1905:

> EDWARD was kind in his invitation to his lodge in Devon, his promise of good fishing in the river was eagerly anticipated – as was the fact that he assured me his groom-loader would be in attendance and would see to our every need. Alighting at the road-edge, the three of us tramped over some very pretty moorland indeed and the vista could have not been bought at any price.
>
> After an hour, I began to realise that the lodge where we were due to spend the night was not likely to have many comforts and on arrival that proved to be the case. My animals abroad have a better roof over their head.
>
> As to the fishing; we cast all afternoon and not once did we even snag our lines which might, for a split second, have given us the excitement of wondering if it might have been a take. At the end of it all, as dusk approached, Edward's man lit a fire and then, with a slight tremor in his timbre, pointed out that he'd only brought sausage and ham, cake and bread intended for breakfast. He had, though, the foresight to bring whisky so we dined on that, bread and cake. In the morning we had the meat and, when resuming fishing, a far better day than the one before.'

Priorities!

In the early 1700s, in the world of fox hunting, the tiny West Sussex village of Charlton had become something of a 'Mecca' for the titled. One particular hunting box, whilst not exactly primitive, was not quite as luxurious as some of those described elsewhere in this book and provided just one main area, at the back of which was a canopied bed. There was though, 'below stairs', a place where a servant could sleep and prepare breakfast. Never let it be said that certain standards were not maintained: records have it that there was also, exquisitely made in best hall-marked silver of the time, a set of six teaspoons, a coffee pot, tea strainer, tea tongs, cream jug and ornate candlestick!

Fox Hall – a West Sussex hunting box. The 'gentleman' would have lived above and his man-servant slept on the ground floor; where he also prepared breakfast

MEALTIMES IN THE GRANDEST PLACES

One would have been well attended to in the grander lodges from which it was possible to daily sally forth in order to indulge in sport offered by the woods, fields, moors and rivers of the surrounding estate land.

Traditionally, the non resident owner or tenant of a grand shooting lodge and his family might well have arrived at the start of the sporting season accompanied by his butler, his valet, his cook, his wife's lady's maid, and his children's governess. The housekeeper, who usually acted as caretaker when the lodge was un-occupied, was generally employed at the lodge on a permanent basis and would be assisted in her duties by seasonally recruited housemaids when the owner or tenant was in residence. At a lodge in Yorkshire, the present cook recollects that in days gone by, there would have been a permanent housekeeper and butler and 'extra help would be brought in for shooting parties.' There was then, no excuse for sporting guests not to be looked after and fed to the same standards as they would have expected at home!

The dining room at Amhuinnsuidhe Castle –
still as it would have been in the Scott era
(*courtesy of the Amhuinnsuidhe Castle Estate*)

For the household staff in the lodge, their day started well before breakfast and one of the first contacts they would have had with whoever was staying, was quite likely to have been the taking of tea and biscuits to their bedrooms. Arnold Palmer described the following in *Movable Feasts* (1952):

'A kitchen maid might have to be down by 4.30am to prepare the *brioches* for the main breakfast table and the trays…to be served in bed. At an agreed moment between 7.45 and 8.15 (and after first knocking)…a maid entered carrying a tray with tea and bread and butter or, disappointingly, a Marie biscuit. In summer she placed the tray beside the bed and then pulled the curtains; in winter she might leave the tray outside until she had pulled the curtains and could see where she was going.'

Breakfast

Accepting the fact that, in the past, shooting lodges were just that – a place to 'lodge' for several days, or even for a whole season – the day would always have started with a substantial breakfast and even today when a place is only being used as a meeting point and a venue for lunch, quite often guests are given breakfast. In what part of the country it is eaten could possibly dictate the likely menu, but there is a good chance that it will consist of good locally sourced food…which is just as it should be.

In that, it is similar to breakfasts served in the lodges of yesteryear when most, if not all of the ingredients were sourced directly from the estate: oats to make the porridge might well have been grown nearby and rolled at the local mill – and the wheat to make the bread ground there. Eggs were laid by hens that scratched away around the stables and out-buildings; in at least one of which might well have been housed a pig for pork sausages, ham and bacon.

Interestingly, the popularity of the typically 'English' breakfast of bacon and eggs coincided with the Victorian heyday of shooting lodges and sporting house-parties and was one of many meat, egg and fish dishes served at the large breakfast enjoyed by people who were going to be outdoors all day. By 1887, bacon and eggs were so popular that Mrs Beeton described it as a 'national standard' dish in her famous tome, *Household Management*.

A gargantuan feast

On non-sporting days, guests wandered down for breakfast whenever they were ready but the 'correct' hour to do so was between nine and ten. If the hosts were out to impress, it wouldn't have been unusual to find eggs, potted meats, fish, toast, rolls, tea cakes, muffins, hams, tongues, pies, kidney, fried bacon and fruit laid out on the sideboard. In the way of something to drink, visitors might have been offered fruit juice, coffee, tea and even hot chocolate.

On a day given over to hunting, shooting or stalking, the food on offer could have been even more lavish and include game pie, cold beef, ham, devilled turkey and game, curried eggs, kippers, mackerel, shrimps, cold fowl, and mushrooms. In order to fortify the 'inner-man' even further, in addition to hot beverages, there was, in many households, the opportunity for a mug of beer or even a glass of cherry brandy (and, if one left one's hip-flask in the gun room or kitchen, it would have been filled with more for later in the day!).

During the summer months, fishermen staying at the lodge might possibly have breakfasted on something lighter before the day's sport, or gone out at day-break to cast their line and then eaten a late breakfast on their return. A somewhat moth-eaten and fox-edged fishing diary bought cheaply at a rural car-boot sale records that the unknown author, was, on the 21st May, 1921, 'out on the river-edge by 6.00am' and 'back in the kitchen frying two fresh caught brown trout at 9.30.'

Lunch

Even on non-fishing, hunting or shooting days, luncheon was usually (but not always) included as part of the hospitality offered to guests at a great many lodges and, depending on the host, could have been either formal or casual in format and etiquette. In the case of the former, everyone could well have been seated by rank but in the latter situation, the gentlemen often served the ladies from a buffet and sometimes any children staying were even invited to the table – remember, it was very much an era when 'children should be seen and not heard'!

On days when sport was planned, participants either returned to the lodge for lunch, or, quite likely, had it brought out to them in the form of a picnic. For those whose chosen sport was riding to hounds, there was of course, very little option other than a few sandwiches in the pocket or tucked into a small pouch fitted to the saddle but, bearing in mind that most packs of hounds met at 11.00am, this was not as great a hardship as it might appear due to the fact that this quite respectable hour allowed for a long, leisurely breakfast beforehand!

Picnics

'There never was an appetite that didn't improve in open air' wrote a sportsman of the Victorian era; a fact that is as true now as it was all those generations ago. For the majority, it will be something packed in the lodge kitchen either the night before or first thing that morning and, for ease of the consumer, food that can be eaten with the fingers is probably best – although there is the long-held tradition on at least one Irish sporting estate that dictates a wide-topped flask of bacon and lentil soup is always carried (the contents of which is served accompanied by oatmeal muffins). The soup is, we believe, known to family and friends as 'Broughdone broth'.

Game pie has been frequently made in many a lodge kitchen – and why not, considering the fact that the necessary ingredients are generally close at hand! Cold, thick-cut slices go a long way towards filling a hungry stomach and are easily consumed as 'finger food'; as are sandwiches, probably the simplest and most popular option. A family friend and frequent guest at one particular northern shooting lodge regularly raids the kitchen in order to make himself a filling of cold, cooked beef, chopped pickled onions and horseradish sauce (all apparently gently liquidised) which he then crams into great chunks of freshly-baked granary bread and, at lunchtime, assures all around him that it is nothing short of 'manna from heaven; nectar of the Gods'!

A picnic lunch on a Scottish grouse moor sometime around the 1920s

An 'alarming' incident

At the London launch of *The Shoot Lunch* (Quiller 2011), a very elegant lady began discussing the wonderfully evocative photo of an al-fresco lunch being partaken on the moors which was depicted on the book's cover. The lady was well versed in the ways of grouse shooting and told of an estate with which she and her husband were involved that still uses ponies to bring the lunch up to the Guns. Apparently (and for reasons that seemingly were considered to require no explanation) she always used to wear a small old-fashioned bedside clock tied around her waist with a piece of cord. On one particular day, just as the pony was approaching with the picnic hampers strapped to its harness, the rather raucous alarm went off … and so did the pony, causing the woman's exasperated but resigned husband to sigh and remark, 'why the hell can't you just wear a wrist-watch like everybody else?' As to when, where (and if) the frightened equine eventually pulled up, no further information was volunteered!

Late lunch

For those who nowadays choose to 'shoot through' and then, once sport has finished for the day, have a late lunch mid-afternoon, it is interesting to note that they are continuing a tradition that started as far back as the eighteenth century. In 1770, James Woodeforde, a Norfolk sporting parson (and there were many of those around at that time!) noted in his diary that:

> I GAVE THEM FOR DINNER a fish of fine Tench…Ham and 3 fowls boiled, a Plumb pudding; a couple of ducks roasted, a roasted neck of Pork, a Plumb Tart and an Apple Tart, Pears, Apples and Nutts after dinner; White wine and red, Beer and Cyder. Coffee and Tea in the evening at six o'clock, Hashed Fowl and Duck and Eggs and Potatoes etc. for supper. We did not dine until four o'clock – nor supped till ten.

Tea-time

Afternoon tea has always played a part in any sporting activity at the lodge – or indeed, any hunting, shooting or fishing venue. The 'beagling' tea organised after a day tramping the fields and ploughland on foot whilst watching hounds on the scent of a hare (or, since the Hunting Act, an artificially laid trail), is still something of an institution in certain parts.

Despite the fact that they may have only had lunch an hour or so before, it would be rare for any team of game shooting Guns to leave their host, or if they are staying overnight, to make for their room without first partaking of a cup of tea and a piece of cake. Modern fishermen too, look forward to a little something in the late afternoon…especially if a sandwich or piece of cake is the only 'bite' they are likely to get. The Edwardian fisherman might well have returned to the lodge for a genteel tea but between the wars there is at least one account of a picnic being taken out on the fishing boat – and fairly hazardous it sounds too. In June1933, thirteen year old Charles Fairfax wrote a letter to his mother in which he said:

> JACK'S PARENTS had the Bishop staying and so we went to the lake after lunch. We fished for trout from a rowing boat and I caught one but no-one else did…at half-past four, we threw in the anchor…Mrs Chance had packed a tea hamper for us all and Jack took out the Primus and got it going so that we could boil a kettle. Jack must have pumped the primus too well because, when he struck a match, some spilt paraffin took light

and the flames started to burn the boat before I put them out with mugs of water. Jack said I should have left them because we could have toasted our sandwiches…

The catching of a big fish calls for something stronger than a cup of tea!

KITCHEN STAFF

Life as it was lived in the lodge has been extensively covered elsewhere in this book but, nevertheless, it is worthwhile briefly mentioning here some specific aspects of life in the kitchen – even if it is only so as to be able to include the fact that there was, included in one particular household, a curry chef from India who used to cook meals with a monkey perched on his shoulder!

In other kitchens, staff behaved in a more orthodox fashion and although servants of one kind or another had been around for a very long time, the Victorian and Edwardian era saw an increase in their numbers: mainly due to the fact that industry and business had created a great many more wealthy upper middle class personages willing and keen to participate in all manner of field sports – and to purchase land and country lodges, all of which required staff to run them.

Interestingly, many of the 'nouveau riche' had little or no idea of what to look for when it came to employing staff; as a consequence of which, books on the subject of household management written by the likes of Mrs Beeton, became instant bestsellers! In *The Servant's Practical Guide: a handbook of Duties and Rules*, published in 1880, the author (identified only as 'A Member of the Aristocracy') had it that '…the manner in which servants perform their duties greatly influences the smooth working of the household machinery, without the constant co-operation of well-trained servants, household bliss is at a risk of being thrown out of gear, leaving the best bred household…at a great disadvantage.'

Twenty-first century kitchen help

Nowadays it would be unusual to find a sporting lodge with more than one member of staff responsible for the kitchen and providing meals for those who visit: in some of the larger lodges this particular task might well be carried out by a permanent housekeeper who acts as caretaker and undertakes some secretarial/administrative duties outside the season. In other situations, it is probably more usual for someone who lives locally to be employed on a temporary basis – or, as seems to be becoming increasingly popular, for the lodge owner to bring in one of the many outside catering groups who specialise in providing lunches for shooting parties and the like. Often they are the most practical option available to any host – irrespective of whether they are intending to provide a sit-down meal indoors or soup, baked potatoes and chilli-con-carne in a far-flung barn. It also has to be said that, from personal experience, outside caterers tend to be somewhat more imaginative in their menus than might be the case with the traditional family retainer!

Some particularly wealthy lodge owners still employ permanent kitchen staff: understandably, those who do, and whom we contacted, were somewhat reluctant to detail exactly how many, and in what capacity, for fear of appearing somewhat ostentatious in these generally cash-strapped times. There is, though, the very valid fact that many shooting, stalking and fishing lodges are now run on a purely commercial basis and, in order to provide the client with exactly what they are looking for, need to have resident staff – their wages will, in many cases, quite rightly, be included in the cost of a stay in such a place rather than come directly from the pocket of the lodge owner.

Romance in the kitchen!

Whilst, in the past, there was undoubtedly romance between the kitchen staff (a situation that was generally frowned upon by employers and, should the relationship ever have become known, could have resulted in one or both of the employees being dismissed – *see also* Life in The Lodge), outsiders seem to have seen the kitchen of a shooting lodge as being a romantic place!

Aubrey Hopwood, an Edwardian playwright, lyricist and author of nonsense books for children, was so struck by the notion that he set a musical called *Sweet and Twenty* in the kitchen of a Highland shooting lodge. First performed some time in the first decade of the twentieth century, the idea for it seemingly came about as a result of Hopwood and his parents enjoying several shooting sojourns into Scotland when he was a youngster.

KITCHEN INGREDIENTS

It is not the ingredients to be found in the cupboards and on the shelves that is of greatest interest here, more the fixtures and fittings of lodge kitchens of the past and present day. Margaret Hutchinson was born in 1904 and, in the 1960s, gave her recollections of living at Moses Hill, a shooting lodge once owned by the Cowdray estate and situated between Fernhurst and Haslemere on the Sussex/Surrey border:

> The kitchen at Moses Hill on the Sussex/Surrey borders (part of the house of which was built as a shooting lodge for the Pearson family at nearby Cowdray Park), was, according to records of the time, 'a large rectangular room with a black range at one end…'

THE KITCHEN was…a large rectangular room with a black range at one end and the washing-up sink along one side…Dinner knives were sharpened and the stains removed on a flat stone on which a paste of red Fuller's earth was spread…The outside of the kettle was always black, though frequently washed to get the soot off. Irons were literally made of iron. They were black and heated on the kitchen range…A cloth was kept handy to wipe them, for they might well be dirty standing there on the range…It is quite astonishing to realise now how clean and white and well-starched aprons, maid's caps, table-cloths, serviettes, etc all came out.

A few miles down the road on the Sussex/Hampshire border, the kitchen of Stansted House – formerly a hunting lodge originally built in the eleventh century but then rebuilt in a far grander style after a fire in 1903 – still maintains the predominantly Edwardian 'feel' and contents. The house was owned by the Earls of Bessborough from 1924 until 1983 and the kitchen there provided many a meal for the shooting parties. This particular example is very much like the ones with which avid devotees of television dramas such as *Upstairs, Downstairs* and *Downton Abbey* will be familiar and has, as its centre-piece, a large pine wooden table. On the table top, all manner of dishes would have been created and it's still possible for the visitor to see mincing machines screwed to the table edge and a set of period kitchen scales. Down one side of the room, in common with most other kitchens of the era, stands a dresser holding pots, pans and ornate copper jelly moulds.

The kitchen at Standsted House as it would have been when it served the family and shooting guests of the Earls of Bessborough

The Magic of a Larder

To have bustled in, flooding it with light would have shattered the magic of the larder. And magical it was. Within those lime-washed knobbly stone walls, bulging and bristling with chunky necklaces of golden-skinned onions...some metamorphosis transformed the glazed-eyed hare, whose cold fur my little fingers had tentatively touched, sending delicious shivers of terror down my spine, into the hot and heady hot-pot; a huge tongue, as from some prehistoric monster, come upon unexpectedly soaking up water in a rose-patterned handbowl, became the creamy pink slices in brown bread sandwiches.

The larder, while seemingly caught in a time warp, was a place of transition: things were always in different stages in the larder; muslin bags hanging from cup hooks on the edge of the paper-lined shelves were draining curds from whey; game was hanging, mincemeat was maturing, and wine 'worked' in the earthenware crocks, while pastry 'rested' above on the marble slab.

June Lewis, describing memories of her childhood in the Coln Valley; taken from *The Cotswold Cook Book* (Global Publications, 1990)

Walls, windows and washing-up

Typically, in the kitchens of every sporting lodge could be found fancy, fluted jelly moulds; butter pats for shaping butter made on the estate; coffee grinders; an assortment of earthenware storage jars and bread 'crocks'; graters and biscuit cutters, and blacking brushes used to black-lead the cooking range every morning. These ranges obviously generated a lot of heat and so most kitchens had high ceilings, with the windows set as high as possible in order to create the most efficient ventilation – not, as is commonly thought, to prevent those 'downstairs' from being able to look out on their employers comings-and-goings.

The bottom part of the walls were covered with vertical pieces of tongued-and-grooved boarding and, above a dado-rail, rendered with plaster which was annually painted with white-wash or distemper. Most floors were constructed of either stone flags or unglazed tiles and, unsurprisingly, could get extremely greasy and slippery. To prevent accidents, scouring stones (known as 'donkey-stones' in the North) and a scrubbing brush were used to help ensure a non-slip surface to floors and steps leading from the kitchen (although the cook would most likely have stood on a wooden duck-board as she worked).

It seems that Margaret Hutchinson's experience of there being a washing-up sink in the kitchen of her home at Moses Hill (*see above*) was unusual because, at the time she remembered, washing-up, the scrubbing of vegetables and all the other activities that might involve water, were done in a separate scullery. A mixture of soft soap and soda was used to wash plates and dishes but something a little stronger such as emery powder was required to clean knives and remove the worst excesses from cast iron pots and pans.

High ceilings, high windows and uncovered stone floors formed the basis of many a lodge kitchen

The all-important bottle-opener!

Household staff could perhaps be forgiven for forgetting some kitchen items when preparing a sporting lunch to be eaten outside...but surely not the bottle-opener or corkscrew? Fortunately, if the gamekeeper was well organised, he might be able to come to the rescue!

In 1878, Richard Jeffries described the keeper's pocket-knife as being 'a basket of tools in itself... The corkscrew it contains has seen much service at luncheon-time, when under a sturdy oak, or in a sheltered nook of the lane, where the hawthorn hedge and the fern broke the force of the wind, a merry shooting party sat down to a well-packed hamper and wanted someone to draw the corks. Not that but what the back of the larger blade has not artistically tapped off the neck of many a bottle, hitting it gently upwards against the rim.'

The modern lodge kitchen

Such a room is, in fact, far more reminiscent of an up-market restaurant than a place of old where all and sundry would enter in full shooting gear, fishing waders or hunting fig – which is as it should be in these days of catering standards, food hygiene and health and safety issues. Look at any website advertising a shooting lodge for use as a temporary base for one's sporting activities and it's possible to see exactly how times have changed.

Most are nowadays equipped with state-of-the-art fixtures and fittings; just a few examples of which, picked entirely at random from such websites, include: 'a well-appointed kitchen (which) provides ample space to prepare evening feasts'; 'satellite TV in all rooms including the kitchen'; 'a warm and welcoming kitchen with flag-stone floor'; 'large kitchen with both a commercial and family-sized gas oven' and, perhaps the most ambiguous comment of all which tells

Modern kitchens which conform to various health and safety regulations are
a prerequisite of guests and visitors to today's sporting lodges

the reader that, 'something of the original mood of the kitchen has been restored' – although on second thoughts maybe the prize for ambiguity (and intrigue) ought to be awarded to the one which simply states, 'no frills, but the kitchen is modernised…and there's shooting and fishing nearby'!

ECHOES OF THE PAST

Even if they weren't living at a lodge all the year round, it seems that some owners didn't stint themselves when it came to ensuring that they and their guests had a good time when they were there! Here, as an example of what we mean, is an inventory of wines, spirits and beer held in the cellars at Eishken Lodge, Isle of Lewis at the time of the owner's death in February 1935.

Champagne: Non Vintage	56½ bottles
Port: 'Crown'	11 bottles
Port: 'Cockburns Vintage Character'	14 bottles
Port: Vintage	2 bottles
Port: cooking	13 bottles
Sherry:	42 bottles
Sherry: 'Narsala'	6 bottles
Sherry: cooking	11 bottles
Burgundy:	11 small bottles
Claret:	10 bottles
Hock: 'Berncastle'	10 bottles
Hock: 'Weiningen'	10 bottles
Hock: sparkling	1 bottle
St. Rock:	1 bottle
Sauterne:	20 bottles
Brandy: 'Hennessy'	2 bottles
Brandy: 'Martell XXX'	2 bottles
Brandy: cooking	2 bottles
Brandy: 'Morgan (old)'	6 bottles
Brandy: 'Grand Champagne'	4 bottles
Gin:	3 bottles
Whisky: (various malts and blends)	41 bottles
Ginger Wine:	6 bottles
Beer	4 gallons

In addition, it seems that the cellars of Eishken Lodge held even more treasures…to whit: 15 bottles of vinegar and 25 tons of coal. All in all, there would have been far worse places to find oneself marooned after an unexpected fall of snow and therefore unable to get home after a sporting foray!

The lodge cellar required a stock of sherry – and there were plenty of companies
ready and willing to supply them. Some even offered the added
incentive of a free bottle to qualifying anglers!

Preparing for the unexpected

Sadly, one cannot live on just the liquid contents of a well-stocked cellar (*see
above*). The estate and/or local farmers might well have supplied much of what
was needed in the way of meat, eggs and milk, but the most organised of lodges
made sure that there was always a good stock of preserved or non-perishable
produce on hand. Quite often these were ordered seasonally from
establishments such as Whitehead & Co. Ltd, who had addresses at 8-9 Lime
Street Square, London, and at Broadwater, Clarence River, New South Wales.

Whitehead & Co. described themselves as being 'Manufacturers and
importers of Australian tinned meats, solid essence of beef, preserved vegetables
and solidified soup squares' and, in July 1876, apparently supplied the following
to Alex D Macleay, a co-tenant of the Grimersta estate on the Isle of Lewis:

96lb of McCollops (possibly an essence of some kind)	@£2.12s.00d
48lb of Oxtail soup (presumably in solidified form)	@£1. 8s.00d
48lb Oxtail in jelly	@£1.12s.00d
48lb Potted mutton	@£1. 5s.00d
72lb Corned beef squares	@£3. 6s.00d
2lb Essence of beef	@£0. 12s.00d

No corner shops!

Finally in this chapter, Geoffrey G. Braithwaite recalls the difficulties involved in obtaining supplies at Kinloch-Quoich Lodge, which he leased for several months in 1926 (the text is taken from Braithwaite's privately published autobiography, *Fine Feathers and Fish*, produced in 1971):

> CATERING was indeed a problem for my wife as the nearest village store was 40 miles away and the nearest town, Fort William, just on 70 miles. She very cleverly solved this problem by working out several months beforehand what provisions, etc. she would need and placed the order with Messrs. Harrods, the perishables arriving at Invergarry station every week, and then one of the cars would have to go all the way down, 40 miles there and 40 miles back, to collect the hamper. Coal was another problem because this came by boat to Kinloch Hourn, about 12 miles away, and had to be carted up a very steep gradient by horse, and the cost per ton, even in those days, was £6.

Coal (or in this case, peat) was required for heat in the lodge and cooking in the kitchen.
Often places were so remote that transport by boat was the only answer
(courtesy of the Grimersta Estate)

BOOTS, GUNS AND RODS

⚜

WHERE, IN ANY LODGE OR COUNTRY HOUSEHOLD, can there be a room more evocative than the place in which the accoutrements necessary for any kind of field sports are kept and equipment cleaned? The smell of gun-oil, leather, saddle-soap and that faint, yet unmistakable whiff of fish-scales and rotting watery vegetation caught in the mesh of a landing net (and which never fades no matter how many times it is washed) are all instantly recognisable and will invariably bring back memories of exploits past.

The older the room, the better the 'feel' and atmosphere: any wood surfaces will, over time, have gained a patina from ingrained oil and polish that cannot be reproduced artificially; in the corner might well be an old armchair – unwanted in another part of the house but too good to be totally discarded – in which countless family dogs have since sat and rested whilst their owners tinkered around doing whatever needs to be done and, tucked away in dark corners, on high shelves, can often be found pieces of equipment no longer used but which are now relics of a by-gone age. Hats, coats, riding jackets, gun-slings and riding crops hang from hooks set around the walls and, in the best organised places, some obvious methodical order can be found.

Glass-fronted cupboards, through which one has to peer through years of ingrained dust in order to see the contents, might be a repository for rosettes won years before by hounds and horses, boxes of flies or fly-tying equipment which are nowadays so brittle that delicate feathers and wools disintegrate on touch, ancient paper cartridges (which should, by rights, be secure in some gun cabinet) and an old fishing reel made by one of the well-known and respected manufacturers. In table drawers – the top of which is the place to lay a disassembled gun, rod sections and bridle parts for cleaning – is often tucked all those things that are not wanted now but 'could just be what I'm looking for' at some later date.

An array of sporting clothing just waiting to be worn at Lees Court shooting lodge, Kent
(courtesy of *C G Hallam*)

RODS AND GUNS

The lodge gun and rod-rooms would probably not have contained the main essentials of sport such as the guns and rods themselves because of the simple fact that they would have travelled with their owner to wherever they were lucky enough to be offered sport! Perhaps a favourite rod or gun of use specifically on the estate where the lodge was situated might have been left behind for future use but generally, a pair of inherited guns, for example, was kept at the owner's main residence. Nowadays, a lodge is likely to be rented out for short periods of the year and the gun cabinets and rod racks be but a temporary home to the tenant's equipment – there is, of course, also the subject of security and the added complications of adhering to modern firearm legislation.

What delights!

The contents of the cabinets and rod racks of the original lodge owners would no doubt make today's sportsmen and women drool with envy: finely engraved side-locks from eminent London gun-makers such as Purdey and Holland & Holland were in common usage, while split-cane rods (made from best quality Tonkin bamboo) and intricate reels from the houses of Hardy, Farlow's and Young's would have sat side-by-side waiting for the next trip to the water's edge.

Advocates of split-cane rods reckon that, even in the world of modern materials such as carbon-fibre, for stream and river fly-fishing, nothing other than a good quality bamboo rod will do! Antique rods are much sought-after, due to which, it is unlikely that one will find any lying unloved and forgotten in the average rod-room. There is an enthusiastic market in the buying of antique reels too: the most commonly found made for use during the Edwardian era were of brass or nickel-plate but the earliest of the period might well have included hard rubber, a material first used circa 1860 and popular for its light weight and durability. Those who could afford them might well have had their reels made of German silver. Some of the very earliest reels (from the 1600s) were created from brass and iron – find one of those at a car boot sale or sporting auction if you can!

However, as far as guns go, there were sportsmen in the past who felt it was the man behind the weapon that was important, rather than the gun itself. E. C. Keith, writing in *Shoots and Shooting* in 1951, was of the opinion that there was no need to worry about the make, length or choke, or the cast of the stock; 'Any normal gun answers the purpose when someone is used to it, provided that it fits and comes easily to the shoulder, and beyond that it is the human element that matters. Whether a gun costs £250 or £25 matters little beyond the pleasure of handling it…'

Most gun cabinets contain an array of sporting 'bits and pieces'…

…and tack rooms, equipment not worn or used for several seasons!

An inventory of sporting equipment

Following the death of Mrs Jessie Platt in February 1935, her executors engaged Messrs Bain & Morrison of Stornoway to make an inventory of the entire contents of Eishken Lodge, the various estate outbuildings and the gamekeepers' cottages for probate purposes. They listed an extensive range of sporting equipment, held not only in the gun-room and other parts of the lodge, but also in the kennels and other adjoining buildings. Here is listed a part of what was itemised from the gun-room:

Rifles

2 Express .380in double-barrel

1 Mannlicher .275in single-barrel

1 Samuel Alport .380in rook rifle

1 Rigby .303in hammerless

1 Rigby .22in high power, double-barrel

1 Holland & Holland .380in rook rifle

1 Rigby .380in rook rifle

1 Webley & Scott .303in

Shotguns

1 pair of Lancaster 12-bore hammer

1 un-named 12-bore hammer, single-barrel

3 un-named 12-bore hammer

2 un-named 12-bore hammer, double-barrel

4 un-named keepers' 12-bore hammer

Firearms equipment and fishing tackle

Quantity of ammunition

Rifle cleaning equipment

Assorted gun cases

4 Trout rods

Spare gun and rifle barrels

Gun cupboard

1 Salmon rod

STUFFED STAGS AND PERIOD PAINTINGS

Also listed in Messrs. Bain & Morrison's inventory of Eishken Lodge were the following:

Trophies of the chase

56 Stags' heads (stuffed and mounted)

2 Stags' horn candlesticks

2 Stags' hoof paperknives

1 Sheep's head (stuffed and mounted)

6 Stags' hoof candlesticks

1 Stag's hoof inkstand

1 Otter foot paperknife

1 Owl (stuffed)

An additional large assortment of various animal skins, stuffed birds and animals.

Trophies featured prominently in a great many shooting lodges – and are an adornment which typifies the classic lodge in many a person's mind. In the West Country, North Yorkshire and the Lakes, otter masks were quite likely to feature:

in the Midlands and in the south, the masks on the shields were most probably those of a fox which had given a good run and subsequently been killed by the hounds.

As far as complete stuffed animals and birds were concerned, the natural world was the sporting collector's 'oyster'. Actually, whether or not an oyster has ever appeared in a gun-room is open to speculation… no matter, wealthy sportsmen with a main London home would, no doubt, have taken their trophies to the likes of taxidermists such as James Gardner, Edward Gerrards, William Frederick Homer, Frederick Selous or, perhaps most famously, Rowland Ward. The latter house is probably best known for their skills in preparing and mounting big game from foreign parts but, for southern Victorian and Edwardian sportsmen, Rowland Ward was a trustworthy recipient of either a previously preserved tiger to be made into a rug, or an owl to be cased. As to having a head mounted (be it bear, buffalo or bison, hare, otter, fox or stag), any one of the above would have completed the task with ease.

No rod or gun-room can be considered complete without the addition of a stuffed fish…

In Scotland – the home of where much that needed to be stuffed was shot or killed, it was the custom to send the 'raw' trophy straight from the lodge to Inverness for preservation, after which, they were sent down to the sportsman's home in London or elsewhere in England at the end of the season. Neither lodges nor taxidermists had freezers in bygone days, so speed was of the essence!

W.A. Macleay & Co., were, along with at least three others, one of the principal Inverness taxidermists and, at the peak of the company's career, claimed to be annually preserving and mounting in excess of 500 stags' heads. As to exactly what period Macleay's were operating from their premises on Church Street; an obituary (printed in the *Inverness Courier* on Tuesday 29th November 1932) with regard to William Macleay (who died at the age of sixty-eight), stated that, 'He took over the business from his father. It is now about 100 years old.' Do your maths!

…or at least one or two deer trophies. The amount seen in this Scandinavian lodge might though, seem a little excessive to most!

Paintings and photographs

It may or may not be a coincidence that a quick trawl through the Internet reveals many outlets in Scotland selling old sporting paintings and prints. Commonsense suggests that such items are there because of the popularity of shooting and fishing north of the border – but there is also the feeling that this glorious abundance might be a result of antique dealers and the like having possibly bought 'job-lots' from old shooting lodges as they were put up for auction or turned into non-sporting private houses.

It would be strange to find a shooting lodge gun-room without at least one old print or painting; a tack-room that didn't depict a horse, hound or hunting scene, or a fishing lodge without a reproduction of a genteel river/fly-fisher combination. Sporting art has always been popular – and originals from the likes of Munnings, Herring and Alken, expensive to purchase. Prints are, however, mercifully cheap and add much to any field sports orientated room. It is perhaps no accident that many aesthetically pleasing prints found on the walls of the majority of lodges are of a typical book size as, during the 1960s and '70s, it was the fashion for second-hand book sellers to buy up cartons-full of unwanted sporting tomes originally published in the early part of the century and then cut out and frame some of the best illustrations for onward sale. Sacrilege to the twenty-first century sportsman and woman, the practice did at least ensure that the finest examples of art remain for our enjoyment.

Evocative photographs from the past, despite being often 'foxed' and

Photographs of people and animals long gone appear in many gun-rooms – and show their personalities. Lady Scott travelled with her Cairn terriers from her London home to Amhuinnsuidhe Castle; the dogs being looked after by kennel attendants
(*courtesy of Amhuinnsuidhe Castle Estate*)

damaged, also appear on the walls of many lodges – but are undoubtedly most prominently displayed in their tack-rooms, gun-rooms and rod-rooms. They are, quite literally, a snap-shot of the instance when, in years gone by, a loader handed over a second gun whilst the accompanying retriever looked expectantly towards the fall of a pick-up; the tightening of a girth by a groom at the meet, or the gaffing of a salmon by a ghillie for his guest rod. For some reason, and despite the somewhat primitive printing methods of the time, there is a certain crispness and indefinable quality in a black and white photograph which is often missing from a modern digital colour image.

There's also a touch of sadness in the realisation that almost all of the people who appear in such pictures are now no longer with us: nor of course, are the terriers, gundogs, hounds and horses that accompanied them.

WRITTEN RECORDS

Pushed away in the back of table drawers or in the darkest recesses of a cupboard, can sometimes be found the incidental notes and records which show how day-to-day life functioned in some sporting lodges: they give a valuable insight into the social history of a given era – as well some very interesting costings. Here are just a few facts and figures plucked at random from an old, rather shabby notebook, which, until it was rescued for posterity, had latterly been used to record milk deliveries! It originated from Dell, a shooting lodge in Inverness-shire, but had somehow found its way down to Liss in Hampshire – it dates from 1946 not long after the property and its environs had been bought by Mr Edwin Beazley from the Lovat Estates …and just a few years prior to being purchased by the then (6th) Earl of Bradford in the 1950s.

Purchase price	£14,550
Purchase price of Ardochy Farm	£2,750
Stocking lakes with trout	£34.18s.9d
Keepers' wages	£35.8s
Tenant's party	£20.00
Casual labour	£2.00
2 days deer-stalking wages	£2.4s.4d
McBraynes'	£0.19s.5d
Keeper's suit	£13.10s
Hire of pony	£2.10s
Keep of dog	£1.7s
Keepers' game licence	£3.00
Heather burning – 3 days wages	£2.3s.6d

NB: When the notebook was first found in Hampshire in the early 1990s, no-one knew to what estate it referred. However, the finding was mentioned in a *Shooting Times* article of 1995, as a result of which, Lady Selena Bridgeman (the Earl of Bradford's daughter) made contact and suggested that the records might be appertaining to Dell. Subsequent correspondence and verification proved that to be the case.

Sadly, Lady Selena died in London in 2001 at the age of only fifty-one and Dell, has, since 2005, been owned by Jeremy Finnis. Dell is, happily, once more at the very centre of stalking and shooting activities. In fact, in the summer of 2012, it was considered by *The Field* magazine to be one of the UK's best shoots.

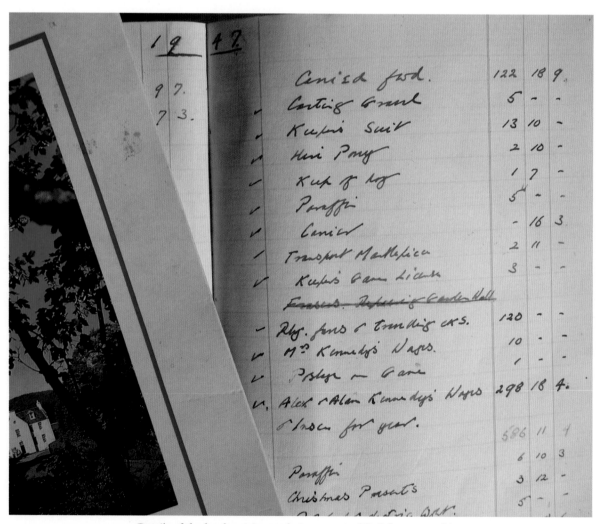

Details of the book entries made in respect of Dell, Inverness-shire

Game books

The Edwardians considered the killing of large bags to be the essence of a successful shoot – and kept records to prove it. A Sandringham game book of 1905 clearly shows a tally of 1,342 partridges taken on the 10th November that year. The 6th Lord Walsingham was known for his love of record bags and would take the keeping of notes appertaining to them very seriously indeed. Not content with a simple game book, his great nephew has it that he tended to register his exploits '…in framed manuscript, with what he took to be suitable illustrations in his own hand – and with evident satisfaction…' How sad Walsingham would have been to learn that his famed and framed grouse record eventually ended up hanging in the lavatory at Merton Hall! Ralph Payne-Gallwey, another well-known sportsman of the era, was also apparently fond of designing and illustrating his own game records for his Thirkleby estate in North Yorkshire – the pages of which contained quite meticulous works of sporting art.

Whilst most obviously not a shooting lodge, Highclere Castle in Berkshire (the location for the hugely successful television series *Downton Abbey*) has, in game books in their archives, information as to how the game shot was distributed after a three day visit there by HRH The Prince of Wales in December 1895. It appears that each of the Guns was given three brace, but his Royal Highness was offered six and, for some unexplained reason, three brace were also sent to the Russian ambassador. In addition, a part of the bag was sent to Newbury hospital and a further fifty head of game to a Mr Horace Voules. Apparently, even the waiters, valets and band members brought in to augment the existing Castle staff were all gifted a brace or two of birds!

Sadly, the average game book tends to get lost or misplaced over the years and with it, the records of times gone by. Avery Newman was born in 1913 into a gamekeeping family and lived at Borden Wood in West Sussex almost all his life. Back in the 1980s, he recollected that 'we used to have game books, the amount of pheasants they used to shoot, but they borrowed them at Forest Mere from my brother and we never got them back again – my old dad was really disappointed'.

Such books are most certainly a wonderful way of reminding oneself of a particular day's sport and, although we all like to recall the 'red letter days' when birds flew well and we shot magnificently, it is also quite interesting to recollect the times when things did not go exactly as one would have wished! One particular event which occurred in 1990 was no doubt recorded in the game

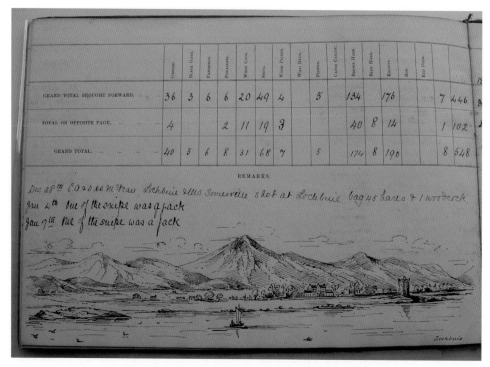

	Grouse.	Black Game.	Partridge.	Pheasant.	Wood Cock.	Snipe.	Wood Pigeon.	Wild Duck.	Plover.	Close Chase.	Brown Hare.	Blue Hare.	Rabbit.	Roe.	Red Deer.	
GRAND TOTAL BROUGHT FORWARD,	36	3	6	6	20	49	4		5		134		176			7	446
TOTAL ON OPPOSITE PAGE,	4			2	11	19	3				40	8	14			1	102
GRAND TOTAL,	40	3	6	8	31	68	7		5		174	8	190			8	548

REMARKS.

Dec 28th Capt McCraw, Lochbuie & Mr Somerville shot at Lochbuie bag 45 hares & 1 woodcock.
Jan 2th One of the snipe was a jack
Jan 9th One of the snipe was a jack

Detail from the game book at Kilfinichen, Isle of Mull

books of those present – and was certainly mentioned in the hunting diary of Tony Harvey, famous for having hunted with over 300 packs of hounds and author of *If St. Peter Has Hounds* (Paul Rackham Ltd 1998) in which he recounts doing so. As a guest of a Scottish hunt, Mr Harvey tells of a day when hounds became embroiled in the happening of a local shoot, causing mayhem and amusement in equal measure: it was, he wrote, '…like something even Surtees could not have dreamt up'.

Hunting diaries

Lord Bellamy, a character in *Bury Fair*, Thomas Shadwell's satirical play of 1689, was of the opinion that the 'strictest order of hunters' were those who 'keep journals of every day's hunting and write long letters of fox chases from one end of England to the other'. From examples perused, the average hunting diary does seem quite a stuffy tome and tends to concern itself more with weather conditions, wind direction, coverts drawn and distances covered 'as hounds ran' rather than show anything of a more human insight. Despite their intrinsically dry nature, hunting diaries are, nonetheless, like game books, important – not only as an *aide mémoire* to those who wrote them, but also for future generations.

What their actual contents might contain is though, obviously a matter for the individual. One particularly grumpy-sounding hunt follower of yesteryear recorded in his hunting diary for 1935, that a day's sport had been spoilt by 'children and farm stock' but failed to elaborate further!

Entries in the hunting diary kept by Brigadier George W. Eden, C.B.E. (a cousin of Prime Minster Anthony Eden), during the 1924 -1925 season are also incredibly brief. Eden – who hunted with the West Street Harriers in Kent and the Cotswold Foxhounds, using either borrowed Army horses or hired mounts – records little more than the venue of the meets and whether or not a fox or a hare was found. His hunting expenditure for the season, listed at the back of the diary, amounted to a total of £30-1/-2½d (£30.06p) for 15 days in the field, inclusive of horse hire at £2/-2/- (£2.10p) per day, cap fees of £8 and various 'miscellaneous' payments.

Positive finds and comments

A diary which yields a little more information is one for 1901 and which belonged to Henry Grey Thornton, a noted Exmoor sportsman (honorary secretary of the Culmstock Otter Hounds, no less!). It includes details of days spent with the otter hounds, the Devon and Somerset Staghounds, Sir John

Henry Grey Thornton's diary records days spent otter-hunting and stag-hunting

Amory's Staghounds, the Dulverton Foxhounds and Mr Bligh's Harriers. Notable 'finds' include a large dog otter weighing 27lb (killed at Chain Bridge on the 5th August) after a 5¼ hour run; 'a capital small stag' taken after a 25 mile run from Worlington on the 28th August, and an 11 pointer killed after a run from Luxborough to Minehead on the 19th September. The diary also has an account of a badger dig at Stockham which yielded a bag of '1 boar and 4 small ones'.

Gloriously positive is the comment made in 1904 by Victorian hunting scribe, 'Dransfield', who was moved to record after a day spent visiting and hunting with the Penistone Hunt in West Yorkshire that, '…there were to be seen such a lot of fine, heavy, large-headed, long-eared, deep-tongued, black tanned and blue and dark mottled hounds as would drive any sportsman wild with delight…'.

Fishing registers

There are also many and varied fishing logs tucked away and forgotten in the oldest of rod-rooms. What evidence of times gone by might still remain undiscovered in the oldest of fishing lodges? As to well documented evidence, one only has to look at the published works of the likes of Oliver Kite who, in 1969, was the author of *A Fisherman's Diary*, in which he extolled the virtue of just being out fishing in the Monmouthshire countryside during early spring – and gloried in the fact that he had been spared another winter.

There's obviously something about fishing that makes the participant feel close to their Maker for, in 1976, Norman Maclean wrote in his autobiographical novella, *A River Runs Through It*, the now oft-quoted first sentence: 'In our family, there was no clear line between religion and fly fishing'.

Some decades earlier, Muriel Foster, a child born of the Victorian era, but who lived until 1963, made, not only a written record of her successful days' game fishing, but also illustrated her fishing diary with some quite exquisite and professionally executed drawings. Muriel's notes and observational illustrations were never intended to be made public and it was some seventeen years after her death before her relatives thought of approaching a publisher in order that they might live on until the present day. More than one person has told us that their rod-room contains a copy of *Muriel Foster's Fishing Diary*!

Muriel Foster might well have had something to say in her fishing diary about this particular notice seemingly banning fisherwomen from the river bank!

From the fishing registers

Historic fishing registers not only contain numbers and weights of all of the salmon, sea trout and brown trout caught on a game fishery each season, but usually include coarse and sea fish – as well as other interesting snippets of information. The 1910 register for Horsaclett Lodge on the Isle of Harris records that various rods landed a grand total of 10 salmon, 89 sea trout, 94 flounders, 41 haddock, 22 lythe (pollack – to the English!) and 16 codling. On the neighbouring island of Lewis, a Barvas Lodge register for 1953 – in addition to listing annual catch figures, also includes a specific entry made on the 15th August stating that the recorder, 'Netted Sea Pool in afternoon and took out 25 fish. 24 were sent to market. Price 7/6d. (37½p) for salmon and 7/- (35p) for grilse – best price ever!' Elsewhere on Lewis, the Grimersta Lodge register entry for the 4th May 1926, notes that four rods accounted for six salmon and four brown trout – adding that departing anglers were unable to travel south after they had reached the mainland due to a 'strike of coal miners, railwaymen and transport workers preventing trains from leaving Kyle'.

Further south, in Herefordshire, the register for the Ashe Ingen Court section of the river Wye records that the Reverend R. Turner, fishing the Lower Boundary Pool, took a catch of almost biblical proportions within the space of one hour on the 23rd March 1922 – landing four salmon weighing 35lb, 32 lb, 22lb and 18lb respectively!

Modern ways for modern days

Although a legacy from years gone by, the keeping of hunting diaries, game books and fishing registers is one tradition that perhaps should be continued by the twenty-first century sportsman. Andrew Bloomfield has designed and sells the 'High Bird Game Card Album' – a hand-made album which contains 40 leaves capable of accommodating up to eighty individual game cards – which, or so Andrew maintains, provides, 'not only a lazy man's record of their days, but also enables the devoted game book scribe to preserve the cards [from] individual estates … which in many cases, have been exquisitely designed'.

NEWBIGGIN & HUNSTANWORTH

The beautifully illustrated front of the Newbiggin and Hunstanworth Estate game card
(*courtesy of James Scott-Harden*)

CARTRIDGE BAGS AND LEATHER-GOODS

In *Come Dawn, Come Dusk* (George Allen & Unwin 1981), Norman Mursell documents his fifty years gamekeeping service to the Dukes of Westminster and remembers that, once the guns were cleaned after a day's shooting, the cartridge bags had to be emptied and cleaned with saddle-soap before being finished off with a light polish. Although emptying the bags obviously made them easier to clean, doing so also prevented them from becoming out of shape due to the weight of the cartridges.

Some cartridge bags had wide openings so as to make loading quicker; others had patented attachments into which one slotted cartridges for ease of access. The 'Gannochy' cartridge loader held 100 cartridges and was very popular amongst those keepers, valets and chauffeurs who loaded for their 'gentlemen' employers.

Gun and loader in action on Ramsgill moor, Nidderdale, in August 1934.
Note the leather gaiters of the loader

Leather boots feature in many gun-rooms and need careful looking after – and careful choice whenever buying a new pair. Sporting writer 'Umbra' writing in *The Field* in 1855, was of the opinion that, on no account should anyone attempt to walk on the grouse moors or hills without some form of grip on their soles, preferably hobnails, 'You cannot walk on smooth soles. I saw a gentleman on Ben Lomond the other day in boots which he called his grousing boots – I should have called them dancing pumps – not a nail in them and the consequence was that he began to slide about very amusingly…' Of course, modern technology has changed the whole way in which boots are manufactured but they still, nonetheless, need to be cared for if they are to remain effective.

Polished to perfection

As far as a hunting establishment's tack-room is concerned, among the day-to-day riding boots might well be found a pair of 'best' boots – the tops of which are light brown over black. The origin of this two-tone effect is commonly attributed to Beau Brummell (1778–1840) as, before he became such a prominent follower of hounds and leader of fashion, most foxhunters, at least according to the Duke of Beaufort in his book *Fox-Hunting* (David & Charles 1980), wore 'baggy long-topped boots with garters coming above the knee'.

Brummell's boots were calf-fitting and had almost white tops. He once apparently told an enquirer that the patent polish on them was the result of using blacking mixed with champagne and peaches. No matter what the truth of that, it is nevertheless, well-known that an equally pleasing effect can be gained by polishing one's boots with egg whites! Furthermore, now that 'easy-care' riding boots made from synthetic materials which are almost indistinguishable from the real thing are available (and far cheaper to purchase), perhaps the best way to obtain a classic finish on these is by spraying them with furniture polish and buffing them hard with a duster!

A trio of perfectly turned-out hunt servants…particularly in respect of their highly polished boots

Despite the fact that the different coloured top of a hunting boot is often attributed to the fashion sense of Beau Brummell, there is another school of thought that suggests the trend originated as a result of cavalry officers turning down the tops of their 'working' boots and thus displayed the lighter coloured leather lining.

That such officers were interested in hunting, there can be no doubt – as indeed were their generals. Beaufort and Morris, writing in 1906, mentioned that, '…throughout the Peninsula campaign Wellington always kept a pack of hounds at headquarters, and chased the foxes as vigorously and successfully as he did the French'.

THINGS QUIRKY!

Possibly one of the most bizarre and obscure things to be found in any gun-room was when, during an inventory undertaken by the National Trust after taking over responsibility for Tyntesfield in north Somerset, they discovered a mysterious hollowed-out and carved coconut 'head'. Although its history is a mystery, Tyntefield's manager, Rebecca Aubrey-Fletcher, agrees that the coconut 'is a strange thing' and says it has 'become somewhat of a novelty item for the thousands of visitors to the gun-room'.

Over the years, there have been many imaginative game carriers invented, bought and discarded – usually in the gun-room! Shot game birds have always been carried by their heads, unlike chickens which are carried by their feet. How strange then, that an auction catalogue entry describes a particular type of game carrier thus:

> ANTIQUE GAME CARRIER, James Dixon & Sons, Sheffield: This antique 'Ghillie' dead game carrier is made out of hard-wood, brass and has leather carrying straps. A thick brass plate, under a short leaf-type spring tension, keeps a diameter opening covered at one end of the device, until it is pressed open. The feet of a pheasant are worked through this opening and then slid down a track, where the bird's feet are held securely in place…this piece should make an outstanding addition to anyone's collection of vintage and antique shooting-related equipment.

In *Game & the English Landscape*, authors Anthony Vandervell and Charles Coles include reference to a 1805 copy of the *Sporting Magazine* which illustrates how, at that time, the practice of shooting flying game was in its infancy. The magazine carried a list of fines which were apparently found prominently displayed in a Sussex shooting lodge:

Shooting at a pheasant on the ground or in a tree	£1.1s.0d
Shooting at ditto at more than 40yds. unless wounded	£ 5s.0d
Killing a hen pheasant	£1.1s.0d
Shooting at a hen pheasant	£ 10s.0d
Shooting at partridges on the ground	£1.1s.0d
Shooting a hare in her form	£ 5s.0d

A sporting room of any description might well have trophies adorning the walls and floors. Frequently, these include items incorporated into what would otherwise be everyday items of furniture and utensils – particularly when it comes to stag's horn. One would expect to see a hazel-shafted thumbstick topped off with a piece of antler standing in the corner awaiting someone to pick it up as they don their boots in order to walk the dog – or to use it as a 'rest' for a rifle when out stalking. You might even think it appropriate to be eating with cutlery, the handles of which one adorned an animal's head; credibility might, however, become stretched when you sit in a chair the legs and arms of which are made from antler and, illuminated by the light issuing from an antler chandelier, you look at yourself in a mirror – the frame of which is made from the same material!

Furniture and cutlery made from deer antler might not be to everyone's taste but a few such objects seem appropriate in the sporting lodge!

OUTBUILDINGS
AND ADJUNCTS

❦

EVERY MAJOR SHOOTING LODGE had a set of outbuildings nearby – usually consisting of gamekeepers' housing, ghillies' accommodation, dog kennels, stabling and coach houses; a game larder for storing dead game birds and fish, and a venison larder and butchery where deer were skinned, jointed and hung prior to use in the house or despatch to a game dealer. Some of the more prestigious were surrounded by gardens which supplied flowers for the household and vegetables for the table and had small fields nearby where cows and bullocks were kept to provide fresh milk and meat. In addition, if a lodge served a large Scottish deer forest, it was not uncommon for a blacksmith's shop to be built alongside the stables in order that the garrons (stalking ponies) could be re-shod as and when necessary.

Further, shooting lodges built in Scottish coastal locations would normally have mooring facilities nearby in the form of a small quay or a floating landing stage to enable the owner or tenant and his guests to arrive and depart by private steam yacht, a mode of transport often far more comfortable than travelling in a horse-drawn vehicle over rough tracks. A number of lodges were also equipped with a fully-crewed offshore steam launch to convey sportsmen to the more remote parts of an estate or deer forest, more accessible by sea than on land.

The situation at Eishken Lodge

Eishken Lodge on the island of Lewis, one of the more prestigious shooting lodges in the Highlands and Islands, boasted an extensive range of outbuildings and adjuncts as well as all of the latest domestic facilities when it was built in 1886. Not only was the property capable of accommodating over a dozen

The outbuildings, keeper's accommodation and adjuncts at Amhuinnsuidhe Castle (the principal lodge on the North Harris estate), were described as follows in a 1925 sales prospectus:

Amhuinnsuidhe Castle Offices
Comprise of a stone and slated building of nine rooms for Gillies, Blacksmith's House, Stableman's House, Joiner's House, Joiner's Shop, Smithy, Coal House, Slaughter-house, Larder, Kennels, and old Byres, excellent Gardener's and Keeper's Houses, and Stables of six Stalls, Harness Room, with rooms over, two Garages for three cars, stone and slated Boathouse. The whole of the buildings are compactly and conveniently arranged around the Castle with a small pier for landing, and there is a bay which provides first-rate yacht anchorage. Above the Castle are attractively laid out Gardens with two Glasshouses. There are five Keepers' Houses in all; at the Castle, at Ardvourlie, at Meavaig, at Bunaveneader, and at Loch Resort.

sportsmen in eleven bedrooms, but also included a drawing room, and a billiard room, be-decked with stuffed stags' heads and other trophies of the chase, together with a large dining room, which, bizarrely, contained a window designed to allow a coffin to be passed in and out! It was, though, perhaps, the subsidiary buildings and surroundings to be found there which makes for the most interesting reading.

Away from where guests might normally venture were various domestic offices: including a kitchen, a larder, a pantry, a storeroom, butler and housekeeper's rooms, a housemaids' pantry, a washing room, drying room, brushing room and a servant's hall. For obvious security reasons – and in common with most other sporting properties – there was a gunroom where guns, rifles and fishing rods belonging to the tenants and their guests could be stored when not in use (and cleaned and put away by gamekeepers or loaders at the end of a day spent on the hill, moor or loch). There were also two safes where visiting sportsmen and their ladies could store their jewellery and other valuables when not in use!

Outbuildings included a storeroom, two footmen's rooms and an additional gunroom used for the storage of ammunition and other commodities. There was also a game larder where grouse and other game birds were hung up on hooks to 'season' before use. Salmon and sea trout were kept on specially made racks or slabs, and deer (either for the house; or for distribution to favoured recipients) were processed in the venison larder.

Slabs or racks helped keep salmon and sea trout cool (*courtesy of M B Macdonald*)

Proper property maintenance

Eishken Lodge was typical of the larger Highland lodges, built with 'new money' made in industry and where the social conventions of the day were not strictly observed, sport being the main priority of the owners and their guests. The facilities, nevertheless, were of the best and set an example to the more traditional landowners, who followed suit when developing estates and constructing shooting lodges and essential outbuildings for letting purposes. Almost all kept their properties maintained to a very high standard, painting and decorating on a regular basis, and installing the latest amenities wherever possible.

THE LODGE LAUNDRY

Every large lodge had laundry facilities of some description in order to ensure a supply of fresh clothing for sportsmen and their ladies, many of whom changed at least twice a day, wearing tweeds while out stalking, shooting and fishing and fashionable dinner attire in the evening. Furthermore, arrangements needed to be in place to deal with household linen, towels, bedding and staff uniforms, all of which were required to be washed and ironed on a daily basis.

Laundry logistics

It was the custom at some Scottish mainland lodges to send hampers of dirty washing away by rail to Inverness or Glasgow two or three times a week in order to be washed, ironed and starched. Only small items such as under garments or baby clothing were usually handled on the premises, where they could be dealt with discreetly. Isolated or island lodges, however, were obliged to operate their own in-house laundry to cope with the voluminous amount of soiled clothing, towels, bedding and table linen produced daily, particularly during the height of the shooting season when every bedroom was occupied.

The laundry would invariably be situated some distance from the lodge in order that views from the windows in any direction would not be marred by lines of washing or continuous columns of steam being emitted by boilers and other equipment. The main laundry for Eishken Lodge, for example, was based in estate-owned premises in the town of Stornoway some twenty-four miles away, which included staff quarters for the laundry maids. Prior to the outbreak of World War One, consignments of soiled and laundered clothing and linen were regularly sent back and forth between the two places aboard the proprietor's steam yacht. Thereafter, things were sent by road transport until the laundry was closed and disposed of in 1936. On the Isle of Rhum during the Edwardian era, the laundry for Kinloch Castle, the Bullough shooting lodge, was situated well out of sight of the castle at Kilmory, some five miles distant – and had its own special motor road connection!

PUMP-HOUSES

In order to obtain a water supply, many resourceful Highland lodges simply 'tapped' a nearby loch or burn situated well above the height of the building itself in order to obtain a gravity-fed water supply. Likewise, some of the more remote Pennine lodges took their supplies from tarns, rivers and streams. It may well be the case that quite a number still use a natural source in this way, but if they do, pumps are now installed in order to fill tanks and ensure a consistent supply for drinking purposes, general usage, central heating and washing machines. There will also be some kind of filtration/purification unit installed for obvious health and safety reasons.

In the past, lodges which didn't have the advantage of gravity-fed water had to find another alternative and, at the most remote of places, water could only be obtained by the digging of a well – from where it was either hand-drawn, or, in more recent years, pumped by means of electricity…itself often difficult to install because of the lodge's great distance from civilisation. One way of getting round this in the early part of the twentieth century might have been to use something like a Petter oil engine with an electricity dynamo system. Before that, steam engine systems provided the first real practical means of pumping but, in addition, not all windmills were in fact mills: some being built for lifting water. A few lodges will have had a hydro-ram.

More or less any mechanical means of generating electricity or pumping water would have needed some protection from the elements and so, at many places, a pump-house was built specifically for the purpose. At others, a pump would have been incorporated into another building: there was, for example, until 1969, one such placed in the back of a goat-shed and milking unit at Robin Hood Hill, a Victorian-built, one-time shooting lodge in West Yorkshire.

The hand-operated well was, though, for generations, an integral and important part of lodge living and, even when a water supply was introduced from the nearest mains, some of the more dyed-in-the-wool workers thought it inferior and were somewhat scathing of the 'piped stuff'!

PROVIDING FRESH PRODUCE

The larger Scottish shooting lodges invariably had a small home farm nearby with a herd of dairy cattle and a flock of hens to ensure a supply of fresh milk, butter, cheese and eggs for the household. In addition, bullocks and sheep were often kept to enable the occupier and his guests to dine on beef, lamb and mutton rather than on a staple diet of grouse, venison and salmon!

Many also had a garden of some description to provide fresh vegetables, fruit and flowers during the sporting season. Usually surrounded by a high perimeter wall and divided into sections by internal walls or hedges to limit wind exposure, vegetable gardens were situated some distance away from the lodge if the ground there was more fertile or better drained, and occasionally contained large heated greenhouses for the production of salad crops, peaches, grapes and other delicacies.

Duncan Macrae, head-keeper and stalker, along with his under-keeper Donald John Carmichael were also responsible for other livestock at Eishken Lodge in the early 1960s (*courtesy of Pairc Historical Society*)

Gardening staff at Scottish lodges, particularly those in the Highlands, tended to be English, brought in for their expertise. Soil was often imported, too – at Kinloch Castle, the Bullough family shooting lodge on the island of Rhum, top soil was shipped in by cargo vessel from Ayrshire to make a garden because the local soil was not considered good enough!

A PLACE FOR WORSHIP

Morning prayers were held on a daily basis in many shooting lodges during the Victorian period and might be led by either the head of the family or by a visiting clergyman. It was obligatory for the household staff to attend, but the gamekeepers and other outdoor servants were usually exempted from such devotions, except on special occasions. A large purpose-built lodge establishment might even include a private chapel, either in the main house or somewhere in the grounds.

Endsleigh, the Duchess of Bedford's family lodge on Dartmoor (built in 1812), originally contained a small chapel – now converted into a bathroom. St Ninian's Chapel, erected in the late 1890s in the grounds of Mar Lodge (once the Aberdeenshire shooting lodge of the Duke and Duchess of Fife), continues to serve as a church, albeit for the local community. Old established ancestral homes and large mansions given over to lodge use invariably contained a chapel of some kind, the religious denomination being dependent upon faith of the owner.

A PLACE FOR LEARNING

Prior to the outbreak of the Second World War in 1939, many isolated Scottish lodges had what was known as a 'side school' attached for the benefit of the children of the gamekeepers, the housekeeper and other permanent staff. The proprietor would provide a schoolroom and accommodation and the local education authority would supply a teacher – usually a student who would stay for one year before being replaced.

During the Edwardian era, at Morsgail Lodge on the Isle of Lewis, the schoolroom and the teacher's bedroom were situated above the stables while the roll-call of the register consisted almost entirely of the children of the head keeper, Kenneth Maciver. At Corrour Lodge in Inverness-shire, there was a purpose-built school, but the teacher lived in part of the lodge. On some Highland estates, gamekeepers living in extremely remote areas were provided with a governess who lived-in as part of the family and taught the children in one of the living rooms in the keeper's house!

GAMEKEEPERS' ACCOMODATION

As an example, at Eishken Lodge, housing was provided for the head keeper and an under-keeper near the lodge itself – four other under-keepers were stationed in cottages at various points in the deer forest. The sixteen or so seasonally recruited ghillies lived in the 'ghillie house' situated in another part of the lodge complex and were looked after by a resident housekeeper.

Everywhere, good quality gamekeepers' housing was an essential pre-requisite if a Highland lodge owner or sporting tenant wished to attract an experienced head gamekeeper – often from the border counties or England –

in order to take charge of his sporting operations in a wet, windy and often midge-ridden environment: indeed, some paid a 'kilt allowance' to encourage the right men to move north and wear the traditional Highland dress for sartorial purposes. That said, keepers' houses built in Scotland during the Victorian period were generally smaller than those in England or Wales and were sometimes little better than an enlarged version of a 'but and ben' type crofter's cottage, or were prefabricated buildings clad in corrugated iron and lined with tongued and grooved wooden boarding. Some prefabricated houses were even tacked on to a lodge in the form of an annexe to save the cost of a wall!

Further south in the north of England, gamekeepers' accommodation at shooting lodges tended to be built in a similar manner to those on large country house type sporting estates. In Ireland, keepers' dwellings varied immensely and ranged from a tiny stone walled cottage with a thatched roof, to a large apartment in the lodge itself.

Head-keeper Charles Grass, outside his lodge house on a Suffolk estate in the 1880s

The ghillie's room

Almost every lodge from which fishing was an option had a ghillie's room of some description amongst the outbuildings. Some were little more than a wooden or a corrugated iron shed where the ghillies met in the morning before being deployed on hill or river. Others were quite large bothy type buildings containing a dormitory, living area and kitchen – sanitation being outside, of course. At Grimersta Lodge on the Isle of Lewis, where a team of ten fishing ghillies were employed in times past, the men, who were recruited on a seasonal basis and drawn from local townships, arrived on foot or by boat early on a Monday morning and returned home late on a Saturday evening in order to spend the Sabbath with their families, living and sleeping during the week in a ghillies' room near the lodge known as the 'Asylum'!

The rod- and gun-room

Although generally a part of the lodge itself, occasionally a room to house guns and rods was situated in the head gamekeeper's house – particularly if the lodge was likely to be unoccupied for long periods of time. This practice still continues on some estates. Sometimes, though, they might have been located in an adjacent outbuilding, but wherever, they were and are, an essential feature of every shooting lodge, be it in Scotland, England, Wales or Ireland.

The rod- and gun-room, (more commonly simply referred to as 'the gun-room' – which is described more fully elsewhere) provides a safe and secure haven for guns, rifles, rods, telescopes, ammunition, fishing flies and other essential items of sporting equipment. It usually contains facilities for cleaning firearms or fishing tackle after use, and often houses game books and fishing registers, filled in at the end of a day's sport.

DOG KENNELS

Sited adjacent to a gamekeeper's house, or in an independent compound, dog kennel blocks built in times past were often quite large in order to house teams of pointers, setters, retrievers, spaniels and other dogs used for shooting purposes (at Glentanar House, for instance, there was, in the 1930s, apparently enough kennelling 'for fifty dogs'). Those dating back to the Victorian period, were often heated by coal or peat fires and

Well designed kennels built as lodge adjuncts in the Victorian era are still in use today
(*courtesy of Sue Knight*)

had a boiler house for food preparation. Some were octagonal in design with a chimney in the centre, one section containing the fireplace and storage facilities for meal, grooming equipment and other necessities.

In addition to gun dogs, kennels at large Scottish lodges with deer forests attached were quite likely to have contained a number of 'tracking dogs' for use when following-up wounded deer on the hill. These were usually deer hounds of some description, collies, or cross-bred dogs with collie, pointer or lurcher blood. Small packs of otter-hunting terriers were kept at some lodges, too, in order that sportsmen could spend the occasional 'by-day' otter-hunting as a diversion from the more serious pursuits of shooting, stalking and fishing!

The kennel inventory taken at one particular sporting lodge in 1935, lists '10 English setters, valued in total at £45 and 2 tracking dogs, worth £4'; while in July 1877, the *Inverness Courier* carried the following notification of an impending kennel sale.

> TO BE SOLD – The entire kennel of sporting dogs, consisting of seven pointers, five setters and one retriever, as shot over in Scotland by G. MacKenzie-Kettle, late of Carr Bridge. The pointers are chiefly descended from Tom Taylor's celebrated dog 'Ben.' See Kennel Stud Book.
>
> For particulars, apply to the owner, G. MacKenzie-Kettle, Esq., Dallicott House, Bridgenorth, Salop.

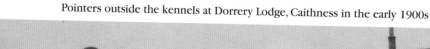

Pointers outside the kennels at Dorrery Lodge, Caithness in the early 1900s

It is almost a certainty that no matter where the lodge was located, behind every one would be a set of iron-railed kennels housing any manner of sporting dogs. In places that were visited infrequently by their owners, dogs might well travel with them or, in some cases, be kept with the estate gamekeeper. Richard Jefferies describes such a scenario in his book *The Gamekeeper at Home* (originally published in 1878):

'A row of kennels, tenanted by a dozen dogs, extends behind the cottage: lean retrievers yet unbroken, yelping spaniels, pointers, and perhaps a few greyhounds or fancy breeds if "young master" has a taste that way.'

Hound kennels

As far as the housing of hounds are concerned there is some disparity. At the main homes, huge packs were kept – and major house architects such as James Wyatt and Sir William Chambers designed their kennels. Sometimes though, these hounds would be taken and temporarily kennelled in far less grand surroundings at hunting establishments many miles away.

Goodwood House in West Sussex was (as has been previously described in *How the Lodge Came About*), built to replace a simple half-timbered lodge rented by the 1st Duke of Richmond in order to follow the Charlton Hunt. When the 3rd Duke took the pack over in the late 1700s, kennels were built alongside the new house. As grand as Goodwood House itself, they were designed by James Wyatt (who was also architect of the kennels at Belvoir Castle and Brocklesby).

Kennels at Goodwood House, West Sussex

Costing £6,000 to construct, the hound lodges themselves were equipped with a piped heating system.

The Duke of Richmond's original pack was disbanded in 1813 and the kennels were eventually adapted as accommodation for staff (and are now home to an incredibly up-market restaurant!). New kennels were, however, begun in 1882 when the 6th Duke decided to create the Goodwood Hunt – structures which can still be seen today.

A kennel for another use!

Tucked well away – for what will soon be realised were obvious reasons – might, as part of the distant outbuildings on some sporting estates, have been constructed a kennel for habitation by foxes!

In Victorian times (and after), although much frowned upon by the purist even then, it was often the case that a 'bagged', 'bag-man' or 'Leadenhall' fox might be discreetly turned down in front of hounds on days when finding a fox in its natural environment might otherwise have been difficult – or if the hunt had an important visitor to impress and wanted to ensure that hounds 'found' not long after moving off from the Meet. Generally caught in the wild as a litter of cubs by keepers and kept in an old stable until required, there were, though, some who almost made a profession of keeping often quite large numbers of foxes in properly constructed 'kennels' and then selling them openly at markets such as Leadenhall in London.

To keep them fit and in condition, 'bagged' or captured foxes were sometimes exercised by a groom or kennel-man waving a brush!
(*courtesy of JMS Pictorials*)

Some of these foxes might actually have travelled some distance. Gloried though a fox was in certain parts of the country, in others – such as Sutherland, Inverness-shire, and Ross-shire, for example – where there was no organised hunting and foxes were shot on sight – keepers regularly took litters of cubs and hand reared them in their kennels in order to supply 'bagged' foxes to fashionable English packs. In fact people from Melton

Mowbray, possibly dealers or agents, frequently advertised in Highland newspapers for gamekeepers and others to send them 'live foxes', not only offering 'good prices', but also willing to pay railway carriage charges!

STABLES, COACH HOUSE AND GARAGE

Sometimes, the adjacent buildings were as grandiose as the lodge itself – frequently, even more so – especially when it came to the housing of horses and, as has been evidenced by the building of the kennels at Goodwood and elsewhere, packs of hounds. Although principal residences rather than properties inhabited periodically for sporting purposes; nevertheless, places such as Audley End, Essex, Peover Hall, Cheshire, Berkeley Castle, Gloucestershire and Seaton Delaval, Northumberland boasted stable architecture the likes of which can hardly be imagined…and all for the sake of appearance.

Even the more modest sporting properties built during the Victorian period contained extensive stabling facilities to house carriage horses, cart horses, personal mounts and shooting ponies used on the hill or moor. The stable complex at a lodge invariably included a large coach house to accommodate carriages, traps and other essential vehicles, a harness room – and apartments for grooms and coachmen (usually situated above the stables or coach house). Many coach houses were later converted into garages to house cars and shooting brakes and equipped with inspection pits plus other maintenance requisites in order that the chauffeur could service cars as and when necessary during the shooting season.

GAME LARDERS

Hollycombe House, on the borders of West Sussex, Surrey and Hampshire was, despite the great place it is now, once a far smaller thatched roofed *cottage ornée* (albeit with eight bedrooms, 21ft long billiard room, library, drawing room, dining room, an octagonal boudoir, conservatory and orangery!) built for Charles Taylor at the beginning of the 1800s. A keen sportsman, there can be no doubt that the house was originally considered to be more of a shooting lodge than a main residence for Taylor and records of the time note that, 'when he [Sir Charles Taylor] first took up his abode at Hollycombe, there was not a pheasant between Farnham and Cowdray, but by judicious arrangement and unsparing expenditure, the estate is now in proportion to its extent one of the best stocked with game in West Sussex – 2,000 pheasants being no uncommon return of the killed in a season…'

Such bags of game obviously required a game larder to be built – and today, the internally octagonal building created for the purpose can still be seen from the public highway.

Essential for storing game of every description in well ventilated, hygienic conditions, the game larder is usually situated fairly near to the shooting lodge, often in a courtyard for security purposes. Those built during the Victorian period tend to be designed with decorative features to complement the surrounding buildings; ventilation grids in place of windows and tiled interior walls and floors for ease of cleaning. In addition, there were fitted racks with hooks from which to hang deer, grouse, pheasants, hares, rabbits and other quarry species.

The Victorian game larder at Hollycombe House, Hampshire

At late nineteenth century fishing lodges, there was a specially sited slab outside the lodge where the day's catch could be displayed (and washed if not done at the side of loch or river) prior to being placed on marble or slate slabs. Larders at deer forest lodges always have a room kitted out along the lines of a slaughter house where carcases, which would be most likely gralloched out on the hill, could be skinned and, sometimes jointed, prior to use in the lodge kitchen or despatch to a game dealer.

These days, of course, in order to comply with E.U. rules and regulations, game birds, fish and deer have to be removed from hill, loch or moor as quickly as possible and hung in an upgraded larder with a controlled temperature of 4°C or lower for small game carcases and 7°C or lower for large game carcases such as deer or wild boar. Further, it is recommended that sporting lodges handling large quantities of game should install a chiller or refrigeration unit in their game handling area.

Slabs kept freshly caught fish cool in pre-chiller days. Grimersta Lodge circa 1930
(*courtesy of the Grimersta Estate*)

In 1860, a certain Frank Buckland had this to say on the subject of game hanging in the larder:

'It is often a difficult matter to know which of a lot of birds hanging in the larder ought to be cooked first…When the birds are brought in after shooting, hold up each before you with his breast facing you, then begin to count his toes from your right towards your left…Let the claws indicate the days of the week. If the bird was shot on Monday, pull the claw off the first toe you count; if on a Thursday, the claw from the fourth toe, and so on. When the birds are subsequently examined each will bear a mark, to show immediately on what day of the week he was killed.'

PIGEON-COTES AND DOOCOTS

Often somewhat charmingly known as 'doocots' in Scotland, on certain estates in the UK, pigeon lofts and dove-cotes were incorporated into barns and other farm buildings around the lodge – although it was far more common for such incorporated lofts to be included in northern outbuildings than it was those in the south of the country. In the southern and eastern counties, brick and weather-boarded buildings looking a little like granaries were built as pigeon-cotes and the birds entered by means of a louvred affair situated in the peak of the roof.

Pigeon-cotes formed part of the outbuildings complex at some lodges (*courtesy of Philip Watts*)

Inside the pigeon-cote were built alcoves in which birds could breed and nest – the squabs
were collected via a ladder which could be rotated around the circular walls
(*courtesy of Philip Watts*)

The idea of keeping a ready source of food close at hand most likely
originated at the medieval manor houses and hunting lodges where stone
constructed circular pigeon lofts could contain several hundred birds which
were, at that time, kept intensively. Typical examples still in existence today show
quite clearly the niches built into the wall, on which the birds would lay their
eggs and rear their squabs. A long ladder that could be moved around the circular
walls from a central point provided accessibility to all the ledges by the person
responsible for the loft and its welfare.

SALMON HATCHERIES

It was not uncommon for the owner of a fishing lodge to operate a hatchery
for stocking purposes. In the first half of the twentieth century numerous
riparian owners experimented with hatcheries, but many gave up after a few
years. The 11th Duke of Bedford had installed a salmon hatchery at Endsleigh
Lodge on the banks of the river Tamar as early as 1901, while at the opposite
end of the country, Viscount Fincastle, proprietor of the South Harris estate on
the Isle of Harris, had opened two salmon hatcheries by 1906 for re-stocking

the fisheries attached to his various lodges. At Shean Lodge in Ireland, the current owners (who have been in residence since the 1940s) still run and maintain a hatchery in order to re-stock their fishing waters.

Elsewhere in Britain, others toyed with hatcheries but, for one reason or another; did not keep them on a long-term basis. Some proprietors were vehemently against hatcheries. Mind you, estate staff were, in some cases, not keen on a ready supply of salmon! In her book, *A Childhood in Scotland* (John Murray 1979), Christian Miller pointed out that; 'Salmon were hauled from the river – struggling on the pointed steel of the gaffs – with such frequency that servants, disdaining the tender pink flesh, insisted that their contracts of service included a clause guaranteeing that salmon would not be served to them more than once a week.'

PRIVATE RAILWAY STATIONS

Although much has already been written on the subject of railways in the pages concerning the logistics of actually travelling to the lodge, it is well worth noting here the fact that, as an adjunct to the Scottish lodge, some of the more prestigious places even had their own private railway station in order to facilitate ease of access to owners, tenants and sporting guests.

On the Dingwall to Strome ferry section of the Kyle line in the West Highlands (opened in 1870), there were no less than three such stations: Achnashellach, built for Viscount Hill, lessee of a nearby sporting estate; Glencarron Lodge, constructed for Mr Shaw, tenant of the Glencarron deer forest; and Loch Luichart on behalf of Lady Ashburton, proprietress of the Kinlochluichart deer forest (who, incidentally, not only gave the land free and paid £100 towards the cost, but graciously allowed members of the public to use her station, too). On the West Highland route to Fort William, a station was built to serve Corrour Lodge when the line opened in 1894, giving the owner, Sir John Stirling Maxwell, and his guests a direct link to Glasgow and thence by overnight sleeper, to London. Elsewhere on the West Highland line, the brewer, Lord Burton, largely bankrolled a branch line from Spean Bridge to Fort Augustus – with a station at Invergarry for the benefit of visitors to Quoich Lodge, his remote shooting lodge on the shores of Loch Quoich, some twenty miles distant. On the Northern Line from Inverness to Wick and Thurso, the Duke of Sutherland had his own station at Dunrobin Castle and even retained a private locomotive for personal use!

Many of the numerous railway hotels that were built alongside stations throughout the United Kingdom, of course, provided lodge type accommodation for sportsmen, particular anglers and hunting folk, who could hire horses and spend a day out in the field, followed by dinner, bed and breakfast. Interestingly, the clubhouse for the Trawsfynydd Reservoir in North Wales, which provided accommodation for visiting anglers during the nineteen thirties, was allocated a special halt by the Great Western Railway on their Bala to Ffestiniog branch line.

ANCHORAGES, JETTIES AND BOATS

As they did with their private railway stations, many wealthy lodge owners constructed excellent mooring facilities situated a short distance away from the lodge where they and their guests could disembark from steam yachts or launches. To facilitate any changing tides, the landing area might well have been equipped with a stone and wooden pier, a concrete slipway or a small floating landing stage – or a combination of all three – and provided an extremely safe anchorage, even for very large yachts.

The private steam yacht was an essential item of equipment for anyone who owned or rented a lodge on a Scottish island or in a coastal location. Built at great expense, and equipped with the latest maritime equipment, these vessels were designed to withstand the rigours of the stormy waters frequently found off the west coast, in the Minch and other sea channels. Crewed by experienced local sailors under the command of a professional sea captain, they not only conveyed the owner or tenant and his guests back and forth from the lodge to the nearest port or railhead but transported household provisions, coal and other essential supplies. Many of these yachts were based in ports such as Cowes on the Isle of Wight, South Shields on Tyneside, or on the Clyde from winter until mid-summer, where they underwent an annual re-fit, and sailed north in July prior to the start of the sporting season.

A sportsman's private yacht near Oban sometime prior to the First World War

The height of luxury

Lodge steam yachts were usually the last word in luxury in terms of furnishings, fittings and other facilities. The *Dobhran*, a 320 ton steam yacht with a 100hp two-cylinder engine, built in the mid-1870s for Valentine Smith, for use at Ardtornish Tower, his Argyllshire sporting lodge, cost in the region of £20,000 to build (approximately £1million today). Sir Samuel Scott's yacht at Amhuinnsuidhe Castle on North Harris, the 445 ton 106hp *Golden Eagle*, constructed to his personal specifications at Leith in 1899, boasted electric lighting – then something of an innovation – and sailed to South Africa during the Boer War to serve as a hospital ship.

The Scott family aboard the *Golden Eagle* in 1906 (*courtesy of Amhuinnsuidhe Castle Estate*)

The Eishken Lodge yacht, *Transit*, a 197 ton commercial paddle steamer with a 75hp engine, upgraded to private yacht standard when purchased second-hand in 1891, was fitted with a flush toilet and an ornate Victorian bathroom. Lower down the size scale, the brewer, Lord Burton, found the 58 ton 20hp *Rover*, a relatively small but luxurious steam yacht, built in 1898, quite sufficient for work in connection with Glenquoich, his Inverness-shire deer forest!

A sad fate
Sadly, virtually all of these beautifully crafted steam yachts were pressed into service during the First World War and converted for military use. Most of those

that were returned to their original owners following the cessation of hostilities in 1918 were subsequently disposed of as they had become far too expensive to run. Small steam launches (a common feature at some west coast lodges and which were kept for local work), continued to be used until the 1930s, when they were replaced by more economical and easily maintained diesel powered vessels or, even, second hand fishing boats.

Small boats for the loch

In addition to sea going vessels, virtually every lodge owned a number of small rowing boats for loch and river fishing. These boats were often permanently stationed on the principal fishing lochs, with a boathouse-cum-bothy situated on the shore for storage during the winter months. Boats were transported by horse and cart to little used lochs as and when required, if there was an access track, otherwise they would be man-handled over the moor by a team of ghillies. Collapsible canvas boats were kept at some lodges for use on particularly in-accessible lochs in mountainous areas, which could be carried comfortably on the back of a single ghillie. Today, wooden rowing boats are rarely found at lodges due to high maintenance costs, glass-fibre boats with outboard motors being used for loch and river fishing instead.

In 1886, the 1st Duke of Westminster acquired the Glendhu sheep farm in order to add more ground to the Reay forest, his Sutherland deer forest, converting the farmhouse into Kylestrome Lodge. His factor, Evander Maciver, recounts improvements carried out to the property by the duke in his privately published autobiography *Memoirs Of A Highland Gentleman* (1905):

The Duke of Westminster added to the house at Kylestrome, improved the garden and offices, built a larder, laundry, and gardener's house, improved three shepherds' houses for foresters, made paths, and erected a wire fence to separate the forest from …tenants' pasture, and connected Lochmore with Kylestrome by a path, built cottages near Kylestrome for ploughmen and labourers, a pier at Glencoul and one at Glendhu, and made this forest as complete and convenient with houses, paths, etc., as he had formerly made the Reay forest.

His Grace now finds Glendhu an excellent forest, and with the advantage of the sea being so close to Kylestrome Lodge, it has become his favourite residence and resort during the shooting season. He keeps a small steam yacht there, which is useful to carry sportsmen to the beats of Glendhu and Glencoul, and also to take parties to Loch Laxford en-route for Loch More. The yacht is anchored in a sheltered bay immediately below Kylestrome Lodge.

A postcard from Loch More during the Edwardian period

CUSTOMS, TRADITIONS AND CURIOSITIES

❧

L IFE IN THE LODGE was not all work and no play for the staff. It was, for instance, the custom in times past for owners and tenants to put on occasional dances, evening gramophone recitals and other entertainments for their employees. On some Scottish estates, the butler and others senior menservants were allowed to fish for brown trout on isolated lochs away from the main shooting or fishing area on their afternoon off.

In the Highlands, in particular, the butler, the steam yacht captain and the head gamekeeper at any large, owned or leased, establishment often belonged to the local Masonic lodge during the early twentieth century: elected to office because of the business which they could give to nearby shopkeepers. They were, therefore, allowed time off to attend Masonic events if their services were not required in the lodge. Generally, though, the customs, traditions and idiosyncrasies of some lodges and their inhabitants make for fascinating reading!

For example, at a certain Scottish fishing lodge, taken initially by Sarah Benedict's grandparents during the 1930s – and subsequently by her parents spasmodically over the years – seemingly originated from the grandparents' time the custom of no-one entering any door (inner or outer) without first of all knocking and saying 'Frederick's here!' Even casual guests took on the custom without question. Only relatively recently was Sarah told that the origin of the saying came about as a result of Frederick, a one-time general factotum, inappropriately appearing unannounced whilst her grandparents were, as young newly-weds, otherwise engaged!

THE PIPES ARE CALLING!

Further back in Scottish tradition – and certainly less personal an interruption than mentioned above – at the larger Scottish sporting lodges guests would wake to the sound of the estate piper parading up and down in front of the lodge, playing stirring tunes on the bagpipes. They would be piped into dinner, too, with the piper remaining in attendance throughout the meal to play a 'Strathspey' or two upon request. The piper was invariably a gamekeeper who was paid a bonus for his extra duties and allowed time off to take part in local piping competitions. Indeed, some keeper/pipers gave tuition in piping as a sideline and organised fund raising concerts for charity!

All-important timing

If a piper wasn't on hand to wake lodge inhabitants and ensure they were not late for the day's events, it was the custom of several shooting establishments to keep clocks set somewhat later than the 'real' time in order to ensure that the tardiest of guests did not hold up sporting proceedings! At Holkham in Norfolk, during the Edwardian period, the then Earl of Leicester kept his clocks running thirty minutes fast – as did the Prince of Wales whilst at Sandringham. At Elveden during the shooting season, clocks were also put forward by a half an hour. Once guests were aware of this minor deception, they must have thought it would have perhaps been easier for the household to start the day's sport earlier and keep the clocks as they should be, but presumably they never questioned the practice for fear of not being asked again!

Foxhounds meeting outside the hunting box (and elsewhere) generally did so at 11.00am. Of course, masters of privately-owned packs of hounds could meet at whatever time they liked as 'he who pays the piper calls the tune'! Northern packs, especially those in the Lake District, might have met at 9.00am or before (and there are a few further exceptions such as those outlined in *Luncheon Lodges*) but usually, an 11.00am 'meet' was, and is, considered the norm. The 10th Duke of Beaufort was emphatic that no follower should be late to the Meet,

A fond farewell
When leaving the fishing lodge for a day on the water, guests might well have wished each other good luck in the form of the saying 'tight lines', an expression still very much part of the parlance of modern fishermen. Followers of hounds have always traditionally greeted the master at the Meet with a polite 'Good morning, Master' – even if, at other times, they are on first name terms and, when an individual left the field in order to return home, it was customary that, wherever convenient, one sought out this particular hunt official and bade him 'Good night, Master' – even if it was but early afternoon. Further, it was considered 'proper' to address a professional huntsman by his surname but a whipper-in by his Christian name…what a social mine-field awaited the visitor to the hunting box!

saying that 'I find it a great nuisance having latecomers arriving from all sides, and I also think unpunctuality is extremely bad manners. "Punctuality is the politeness of Princes" is by no means an idle saying…'

SPORTS AND SOCIAL EVENTS

In times past, owners and tenants of Scottish shooting lodges often organised sporting activities or social events for the local community. At Knoydart in Inverness-shire, the proprietor, Edward Salvin Bowlby of Gilston Park, Hertfordshire (from where he was also a Joint-Master of the Essex Foxhounds), inaugurated an annual Highland Games for his staff and crofting neighbours followed by a supper and dance. In 1897, to celebrate Queen Victoria's Diamond Jubilee, Bowlby presented each child on the estate with a commemorative mug and entertained his servants and tenants to a dinner and dance, sending his steam yacht all along the coast in order to collect those living in remote locations.

On the Isle of Rhum at Kinloch Castle (the principal shooting lodge), Sir George Bullough, not only provided a staff recreation hall complete with badminton, billiards and table tennis facilities, but also organised an annual picnic and football matches between the crew of his yacht, the *Rhouma* and his three staff teams. Similarly, on the Isle of Lewis, Lady Dorothy D'Oyly Carte (husband of opera impresario, Rupert D'Oyly Carte), tenant of the Soval estate during the 1920s and '30s, encouraged the local boys to play football, presenting the 'Lady Dorothy D'Oyly Carte Cup' to the Island Football League in 1923.

Elsewhere, some of the larger Scottish lodges, particularly those in sheltered locations boasted a tennis court or a croquet lawn – but these were, it must be admitted, provided as an alternative form of sport for their guests rather than their employees.

The billiard room at Amhuinnsuidhe Castle (*courtesy of the Amhuinnsuidhe Castle Estate*)

The Ghillies' Ball

The highlight of the shooting lodge year was the end of season 'Ghillies' Ball' or dance organised by the owner or the sporting tenant, a tradition which still continues today on a number of large Scottish estates On these occasions, the estate staff, local tradesman, neighbouring farmers or crofters and others involved with the shooting and fishing activities were invited to a grand dinner and ball in the lodge, where they danced and dined on an equal footing with sportsmen and their wives. In addition to providing a ball and dinner, some owners and tenants would also put on a fishing competition for the keepers and ghillies, presenting cash prizes to the winners, give a substantial sum of money for the benefit of the poor in the district, distribute food parcels amongst the sick and elderly and pay for a sumptuous tea for the children at the local school.

On the Dukes of Westminster estate at Lochmore, Sutherland, a Ghillies' Ball was always held. Stalkers, gamekeepers and ghillies would all be welcomed by their employer before being immediately offered a glass of whisky in the dining room. Their wives were, however, welcomed by the Duchess in her private sitting room and after this segregated reception was over, a traditional Highland Ball would commence…with all the customary skirl of bagpipes, dance music and reels.

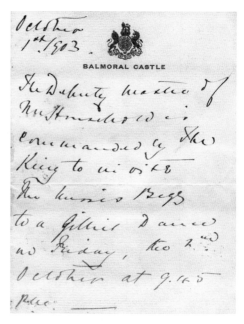

A personal invite to the Ghillies' Ball of 1903 at Balmoral

An 'end of season' report from the *Oban Times*, 1898.

Glenquoich Lodge
Lord and Lady Burton and guests have left Glenquoich for the South – Deer stalking was brought to a close on the 6th.Inst., and, not withstanding the very short season, 115 stags fell to the rifle of his Lordship and his friends, which included several good heads, particularly one of 14 tines, one 10 pointer, and an unusually wide head of 39 inches, all of which have been sent to Inverness for preservation. The season this year has been an unusually busy one, owing to the large number entertained, which included several distinguished guests. – The Ghillies Supper and Ball was held on Wednesday night last week, when a most enjoyable evening was spent by all.

Hunt Balls

Scotland and its stalking, fishing and shooting community had its ghillies' balls and other end-of-season get-togethers but in the Shires and southern counties, the Hunt Ball took pride of place – and was, if the owner could be persuaded, traditionally held in one of the larger hunting boxes, or at a master's country residence. Somewhat tongue in cheek, author Willie Poole – himself a MFH, made the following observation in *Hunting – An Introductory Handbook* (published by David & Charles in 1988): 'The great coup is for the organisers of some stately home to host the frolic. Owners of stately homes, however, tend to be wary of accepting such an honour, for hunting people take seriously the business of enjoying themselves. Some 350 hunters enjoying themselves is not a thing to be considered lightly…'

Despite searching through many hunting books written during the late Victorian and Edwardian era, comments of a more serious nature are difficult to find and, apart from the observation from Sir William Beach Thomas, who opined that 'the Hunt Ball is the gayest and most regular of social events', scribes of the time seem far more preoccupied by the important business of hound breeding and hunting itself!

PLACES AT THE TABLE

The numbers of people sitting down at any sporting occasion is likely to vary. How often, for example, has the modern-day shoot captain been asked by whoever is responsible for the lunch to ascertain how many will be sitting around the table? Most often done for practical, administrative reasons, should, after a head-count, the number be thirteen, the superstitious host might well consider their options!

Having thirteen people around a table is thought by many to be extremely unlucky – the origins of which have all to do with Jesus and the Last Supper… at which He was betrayed by the thirteenth member of the group. 2,000 years on, more than one shooting host has refused to allow even thirteen close friends to sit around their table and have, variously, brought in a loader or beater to make up an even number, banished the shoot captain to either the kitchen, or to eat with the loaders and beaters, or, in one case we know of in East Sussex, actually had an extra place laid and sat a child's teddy-bear at the table!

MEN ONLY!

In period paintings of the eighteenth and early nineteenth century, there is often illustrated a group of men dressed in hunting attire – usually sprawled out smoking a pipe and drinking – the title of which is usually something along the lines of 'A Group of Huntsmen', or, 'Gentlemen after a day's sport'. Such paintings show that it was common-place for the men to retire to an inn or to a male-only part of the house in order to relax and talk about the day's events. This tradition was adopted by many fishing and shooting residents of the sporting lodge where the men-folk would either go to their fire-warmed study armed with a glass of whisky and a cigar in order to fill in their game book, or meet together after the evening meal in something of the atmosphere of a London club.

Gentlemen often retired to the lodge library after a hard day's sport

No matter whether the participants' chosen sport be shooting or hunting (fishing, being considered somewhat more genteel, seems to be missing from any accounts we have read!), things might have got a little out of hand in the lodge or hunting box – as can be evidenced by Siegfried Sassoon's account in his classic *Memoirs of a Fox-hunting Man*:

> AFTER DINNER we moved into the other room, which was even smaller.
> A decanter of port quickly became empty, and a certain rowdiness began
> to show itself among the company, though there was nothing to be
> rowdy about and very little space to be rowdy in. When Henry brought
> in the replenished decanter Jack picked up a small tumbler and filled
> it…A few minutes afterwards he threw a chair across the room and the
> other young men felt it incumbent on them to imitate him. He then

refilled his glass with port, standing in the middle of the room, drank it straight off, and collapsed on the floor. The little room was overheated by a roaring fire, and the air was heavy with cigar smoke.

CARE IN THE COMMUNITY

It was not uncommon in the pre-Welfare State era for sporting visitors to help their less well off neighbours either financially or in kind. Many gave surplus venison, salmon, hares and other game to the nearest hospital or poor law institution. Some sent money to the local minister or poor law official so that they might buy coal or provide food parcels for those in impoverished circumstances. Others paid for a sumptuous tea for the local school children and a substantial Christmas dinner for the elderly. Harry Holmes, a wealthy London insurance underwriter, who leased the Uig Lodge estate on the Isle of Lewis from 1908 until 1913, not only distributed venison to each family in the district at the end of the stalking season and gave them 1lb of sugar and 6lbs of tea each Christmas throughout the period of his tenure, but also sent twice weekly supplies of wine, soup and pudding to sick and needy members of the community.

Sportsmen helped the community in other ways, too, providing funding assistance for capital building projects. Mr Barclay, tenant of Newtonmore grouse moor in the 1890s, donated £25 towards the cost of building a public hall and library at Newtonmore. In 1898, Lord Burton, lessee of Glenquoich Lodge in Inverness-shire, extended the public road at Kinloch Hourn and constructed a new pier at Skearry at his own expense to provide mooring facilities for his steam yacht and local vessels. Mr Joseph Platt of Eishken Lodge on the Isle of Lewis subscribed £100 annually to the Lewis hospital during the early Edwardian period, thus enabling the hospital to be upgraded on a regular basis. Mr Platt also encouraged his sporting guests to visit the hospital and make a donation to the funds. Obviously keen on medical matters, he always had a doctor in his shooting parties, both as insurance against firearms accidents and to provide free advice and treatment for local people!

Despite his somewhat austere appearance, Joseph Platt was a well-known and much liked benefactor in the Highlands and Islands (*courtesy of K R Mackay*)

The season at Langwell
In 1899, the *Inverness Courier* carried the following 'End of Season Report'.

The Duke and Duchess of Portland left Berriedale for London yesterday, the Marquess of Tichfield and Lady Victoria Bentinck accompanying them. On Monday night the Duke and Duchess of Portland entertained their ghillies, servants, and neighbours to supper and dance on the conclusion of the season's sport at Langwell Forest, Berriedale. The season was one of the best for years. Grouse and other winged game were plentiful and healthy: the stags have been exceptionally good; there were several royals and the weights were splendid. Including the Duke and Duchess of Connaught, there was a large and distinguished company at Langwell this season. After supper, the health of the Duke and Duchess was drunk with the greatest enthusiasm. His Grace said in reply, that he was well pleased with the season's sport, and was soon to leave the Highland home he loved so well.

TIPPING

Tipping has been an established practice at most sporting lodges since the Victorian period. Individual sportsmen have traditionally given a cash gratuity at the end of their visit, not only to keepers and ghillies who have served them, but also to members of the domestic staff. In times past, some lodge owners and tenants kept a 'tip box' and encouraged guests to put money in there rather than to give it to particular employees – the money thus accumulated was then distributed equally between the staff at the end of the season. Other lodges set 'tipping scales' to ensure that their employees were tipped according to their rank. For example, in 1962, Lord Baillieu, chairman of the angling syndicate who owned Grimersta Lodge, recommended that each rod should tip the head keeper £1 per week, the head ghillie 15/- (75p), the second ghillie 10/- (50p), the cook 12/6d. (62½p), and the kitchen maid 7/6d (37½p). Individual ghillie bonuses at this time were 10/- for ten salmon caught in one day by a single rod, £1 for fifteen salmon and £1-10/- for twenty salmon.

The Gamekeeper magazine, dated May 1907, included a sample scale of tips paid by guests at Scottish shooting lodges

Butler £1
First footman 10/-
Chauffeur 10/-
Head keeper (grouse) £1
Second keeper 10/-
Head stalker (deer forest) £3
Second stalker 10/-
Fisherman (ghillie) £1

This is a very moderate estimate. Many head stalkers expect and receive a £5 note if the guest is lucky enough to kill one or two stags.

As far as hunting in the south was concerned, in 1936, David Brock urged newcomers to fox-hunting to remember that the wages of professional hunt staff were out of all proportion to the hours of work they did, and for the risks they undertook. Therefore, the custom and tradition of giving them a Christmas 'box' should always be rigorously upheld – as he quite correctly noted: 'If you can afford to keep a horse and hunt at all you can surely afford a pound note for the huntsman and a ten shilling note for each whipper-in.'

QUIRKY CUSTOMS

Occasionally a lodge might have its own unusual customs and rituals. For example, at Kinloch Castle, the Bullough family shooting lodge on the Isle of Rhum, Sir George Bullough, built a range of hot houses during the early twentieth century, one of which contained a heated turtle pool for turtle rearing – apparently Rhum turtle soup was an 'excellent restorative' after a hard day on the hill! At Glenkirk Lodge in Inverness-shire, the tenant, the Reverend E.L. Browne, head master of an Eastbourne private school, had his own special method of drying out wet shooting boots, filling them with hot oats – on the basis that the oats dried the boots from inside and by swelling, prevented them from shrinking.

At Bragleenbeg Lodge, in Argyll, during the Edwardian era, the thrifty owner apparently insisted that guests for the winter shootings, who were billeted in a farmhouse, could only eat what they caught – the meals consisting of brown trout, porridge and bacon for breakfast and hare soup, sea trout and grouse or pheasant for dinner on a daily basis for a fortnight or more, no variation being permitted. Elsewhere, at one un-named Dumfries-shire lodge during the late Victorian period, it was apparently the practice for bottles of beer to be placed in pools in burns or in small lochans throughout the moor immediately prior to the 'Glorious Twelfth' in order that the thirsty tenant and his guests could regularly fortify themselves as they walked-up grouse on the great day!

Traditional tweeds and stuffed stags

The larger shooting lodges, of course, traditionally had their own dedicated stalking tweeds, designed so that they would blend in with the local ground in order to act as a 'camouflage suit' when worn by sportsmen in pursuit of deer. It was the custom at virtually every lodge with a deer forest attached for the best heads to be 'preserved' (stuffed and mounted on an inscribed shield) in order that they could grace the walls of the lodge, the stalker's London home, or his English country seat. Heads were usually sent to one of the several Inverness taxidermy companies for preservation, then sent south by train to the owner in a finished state. During the Edwardian period, W.A. Macleay & Co., one of the top Inverness taxidermists, claimed to preserve in excess of 500 stags' heads annually – charging an average of £1-15/- (£1.75) to stuff and mount a head on an oak shield.

The all-round sporting supplier circa 1930 – to include a taxidermy service!

A good excuse for a drink!

It used to be a regular occurrence that a litter of puppies born to a Northern hunting establishment participated in a christening ceremony where drink (often a mixture of local ale and whisky) was poured into rather ornate silver or glass punchbowls and the pups either anointed or completely dunked. Custom then dictated that members of the hunt would then be invited to partake of the contents of the bowl. Still carried out in certain places but slightly more sanitised in this day and age, old newspaper cuttings and records suggest that christenings have been going on in sporting pubs and at hunting boxes since at least 1860.

Whether the title and chorus of Victorian hunting enthusiast, George Whyte-Melville's well-known song is referring to a puppy christening is open to doubt: nevertheless, it encompasses a certain sentiment when it declares; *Then drink, puppy drink,/And let every puppy drink/That is old enough to lap and to swallow,/For he'll grow into a hound/So we'll pass the bottle round,/And merrily we'll whoop and we'll holloa.*

THE 'MACNAB' CHALLENGE

Another good excuse for a drink would be if you managed a 'MacNab'. Some Scottish shooting lodges still offer guests the opportunity to participate in the MacNab Challenge; an activity which involves catching a salmon, shooting a brace of grouse and grassing a stag, all within the space of one day. Thought originally to have been devised by the author John Buchan, for his adventure novel *John MacNab* (published in 1925), the 'challenge' has been an integral part of the Scottish sporting scene for the past seventy years or so, and currently takes place on a number of well known estates – mainly in the Highlands and Islands.

The MacNab Challenge is particularly popular in the Outer Hebrides, not only at Amhuinnsuide Castle, but also on various estates on the Isle of Lewis including Aline and Scaliscro. In fact, Scaliscro made the news headlines in 1988 when cricketing legend, Ian Botham, achieved his first 'MacNab' there on the 5th of October that year.

The Isle of Lewis also offers 'The Isle of Lewis MacNab', which involves 'Shooting a brace of grouse, catching a salmon, and shooting a stag, in an honourable and sportsmanlike manner, within a twenty-four hour period on the Isle of Lewis'. This version of the MacNab challenge takes place over three

A successful MacNab! (*courtesy of Cree MacKenzie/Scaliscro Lodge Estate*)

estates; Scaliscro, where a brace of grouse are walked-up and shot over pointer dogs, Eishken, where a stag is stalked and grassed, then extracted with a pony and, finally, Uig Lodge where a salmon is caught by rod and line on the evening rise on the Fhorsa river.

In addition to the Outer Hebrides, properties on the mainland currently offering the opportunity for sportsmen to undertake a 'MacNab' include the 35,000 acre Kinlochewe and Lochrosque estate in Ross-shire, Kinloch in Sutherland, and Aberchalder in Inverness-shire. Although very popular, particularly with younger sportsmen, the MacNab is not always a cheap challenge, with some landowners and corporate event organisers charging fees of up to £1,500 per person per day for each attempt!

An itemised bill made out to 'Thomas Bailey Forman, Esq., of Wilford, Nottinghamshire' in July 1925, for a month's fishing at Grimersta Lodge, Isle of Lewis.

Board and lodging	£31-10/-
Use of lodge car and chauffeur	£ 4-11/-5d
Whisky	£ 9-10/-6d
Whisky for ghillies	£ 3-7/-6d
Cocktails	13/-6d
Wine	£12-11/-4d
Soda Water	£ 1
Laundry	8/-2d.
36 fish mats	£ 1-18/-
50 salmon (249 lbs @ 2/-)	£24-18/-
15 salmon (93 lbs. @ 2/-)	£ 9-6/-
Matches	2/6d
Box for salmon	5/-
Total	= £100-1/-11d

ROMANCE AT THE LODGE

Keen to make their shooting lodge pay its way, a number of Scottish lodge owners have, in recent years, secured a wedding licence, thus enabling couples to marry in a unique environment and then hold their wedding breakfast in luxurious surroundings. Tulloch Castle near Dingwall in Ross-shire (now a hotel), Amhuinnsuidhe Castle on the Isle of Harris and Tulchan Lodge on Speyside, all offer this facility – the latter in its own estate church. By doing so, they are, one supposes, creating something that will rapidly become a custom associated with sporting lodges for future generations. In the past, though, things were somewhat different as regards marriage!

Bettering oneself!

As we said at the outset of this particular chapter, it was not all work and no play for some of the resident lodge staff or outdoor employees and sportsmen have occasionally fallen in love with lesser mortals while staying in a shooting lodge!

Francis Hemming, a wealthy bachelor and heir to a West Midlands needle manufacturing fortune, rented Eishken Lodge on the Isle of Lewis in the 1870s and married the estate farm manager's daughter, Jane Hymers, in 1874 (the ceremony being performed in the lodge by the local Free Church minister), a move that ultimately led to him being disinherited by his family and being left penniless for the remainder of his life! Alexandra MacKenzie, another local Lewis girl fared somewhat better: after marrying the ultra-rich Lancashire textile machinery magnate, John Bullough, tenant of the Uig Lodge shootings, in 1884 (as his second wife), she not only became chatelaine of the White House on the Isle of Rhum and of Meggernie Castle in Perth-shire, but also of the Bullough family seat, the Rhyddings, at Oswaldtwisle in Lancashire!

Wedding celebrations at Glenquoich Lodge

Great rejoicings took place at Glenquoich Lodge on 31st January1894, to celebrate the marriage of Lord Burton's daughter and sole heiress, the Honourable Nellie Bass, to James Baillie of Dochfour, an Inverness-shire laird. Around 100 tenants and employees from Glenquoich and the adjoining deer forest of Glenkingie were entertained to drinks in the lodge billiard room at the appointed hour of the wedding (which took place elsewhere), while a further 150 were provided with a supper in the evening followed by pipes and dancing in the ballroom until the small hours. Outside, a lavish firework display was put on for the guests by a London firm of pyrotechnists, and a chain of bonfires was lit from Glenquoich to Invergarry.

THE VISITORS' BOOK

During the late Victorian and the Edwardian periods, in keeping with the best country house traditions, the owners and lessees of the more prestigious lodges maintained a visitors' book, inviting guests to enter their name, rank and address, and wherever possible to contribute comments about the quality of sport, make sketches or watercolour paintings of lodge life, or to write suitable verses.Those that still survive now provide valuable social and historical information about a bygone era, as well as being collector's items.

As an example, the visitors' book kept by the Victorian engineer, Sir John Fowler, and his successors at Braemore Lodge in Ross-shire (demolished by explosives in the 1950s!) contained sketches by Sir Edwin Landseer, R.A., Sir John Everett Millais, R.A., Lt-General Henry Hope Crealock and other distinguished artist-stalkers as well as various literary contributions by Sir William Harcourt, William Russell and others and contained the signatures of some of the leading men of the day.

Alfred Gathorne-Hardy, who visited Braemore as the guest of Sir John Fowler on a number of occasions during the late nineteenth century, records some details about the book in *My Happy Hunting Grounds*, published in 1914:

> THE WHOLE VOLUME is full of interest with its mementoes and autographs of the numerous soldiers, statesmen, churchmen, and leaders of science who enjoyed the hospitality of the great engineer. The names of Lord Strathnairn and Earl Roberts, Archbishops Benson, Maclagan, Thomson, and Magee, Professor Owen, Sir Frederick Murchison, and many other great men of the Victorian age are to be found in its pages.

Interestingly, in her book *A Countrywomans' Year*, published in 1973, Georgina Rose refers to a Scottish lodge which kept a visitors' book for dogs – containing comments such as 'Blue hares too fast.' (Which lodge we wonder?)

Braemore Lodge, which was, until it was demolished in the 1950s, home to a wonderful visitors' book containing the names and sketches of several noted artist-stalkers

V I P visitors

Shooting lodges have accommodated more than their fair share of important guests over the years, ranging from royalty, aristocracy and politicians to financiers, captains of industry and leading figures from the world of sport. King Edward VII regularly stayed with Lord Burton at Glenquoich Lodge for deer stalking and with Sir Phillip Sassoon at Tulchan Lodge for grouse shooting. His nephew, the German Kaiser was a guest at Tulchan and Glencalater Lodges, leaving a £20 tip for the gamekeepers at the former property. The early twentieth century cricketing legend, Charles Basil Fry, spent fishing holidays at lodges on both North and South Uist in the Outer Hebrides – his ghillie, Ewan Macdonald, even named a son, 'Charles Basil Fry Macdonald' in his honour.

Mary, 11th Duchess of Bedford, the pioneer aviator and bird watching enthusiast, rented a lodge and shootings on the Island of Barra prior to the outbreak of the Great War in 1914 in order to study birdlife and to shoot wildfowl. Sir Winston Churchill is said to have stayed in various Speyside lodges in order to fish for salmon, and was often accompanied by his personal physician Lord Moran. It goes without saying, of course, that numerous well known American millionaires have become lodge devotees, especially those with Scottish roots!

Literary guests

From time to time, various well known authors have sought refuge in the secluded sanctuary of an isolated shooting lodge, particularly those with the ability to combine writing with angling. The Scottish playright, Sir J.M. Barrie, creator of 'Peter Pan', conceived his famous drama 'Mary Rose', while fishing on Loch Voshimid on the Amhuinnsuidhe Castle estate just after the end of the Great War. Arthur Ransome – another keen angler – spent the summers of 1945 and 1946 at Uig Lodge on the Isle of Lewis while researching and writing his novel, *Great Northern*; the final volume in his *Swallows and Amazons* series of children's books.

Former poet laureate, the late Ted Hughes was a regular visitor to Grimersta Lodge (another Lewis sporting property), and penned verses for members of the staff. Lt.-General Henry Hope Crealock, the great Victorian deer stalking artist and author, stayed in numerous shooting lodges throughout the Highlands when collecting material for his classic book *Deer Stalking in The Highlands of Scotland* (published in 1892). Lancelot Speed, a leading Victorian artist and book and magazine illustrator, broke new ground while spending the late summer and autumn of 1885 as the guest of Sir Arthur Bignold, M.P., at Strathbran Lodge in Ross-shire, by writing a light hearted illustrated book about his experiences on hill, moor and loch – aptly titled, *A Sojourn in The Highlands*.

Politics and politicians

Many lodges have political connections, having hosted sporting Members of Parliament and Cabinet Ministers at one time or another. However, Scaliscro Lodge on the island of Lewis, must be one of the few lodges to have been used as an election campaign headquarters! The late Right Honourable Iain Macleod, P.C.,M.P., a son of the owner, Dr Norman Macleod, began his political career from the lodge when he un-successfully stood as Conservative candidate for the Western Isles in the General Election of 1945. Undaunted by a small poll, Macleod later secured the seat of Enfield West and rose to become Secretary of State for the Colonies, Leader of the House of Commons, and Chairman of the Conservative Party from 1961until1963.A keen sportsman in his younger days, Macleod had spent his school holidays at Scaliscro, catching trout and salmon and shooting walked-up grouse over Gordon setters.

A guest preparing to leave – but presumably, not before having signed the visitors' book!
(*courtesy of the Amhuinnsuidhe Castle Estate*)

While not directly connected with staying at a sporting lodge, the following poem, written around the cross-over period of the Victorian and Edwardian eras, does, perhaps, still hold true today!

The Perfect Guest

She answered by return of post
The invitation of her host
She caught the train she said she would
And changed at junctions as she should
She brought a small and lightish box
And keys belonging to the locks
Foods, rare and rich, she did not beg,
But ate the boiled or scrambled egg
When offered luke-warm tea she drank it
And did not crave an extra blanket
Nor extra pillows for her head
She seemed to like the spare room bed
She brought her own self-filling pen
And always went to bed at ten
She left no little things behind
But stories new and gossip kind.

Edward Verrall Lucas (1868–1938)

GHOSTS OF THOSE WHO HAVE GONE BEFORE

Unsurprisingly, the isolation and often gloomy, daunting appearance of many lodges has lead to the belief that they are haunted – and nowhere more so than in Scotland. There is, for instance, at Edinbane on the Isle of Skye, 'The Lodge' which used to be a sixteenth century hunting lodge (and is now a hotel), in the grounds of which were, at some time, hung criminals whose spirits are said to still remain. At Glamis Castle, best known as being the home of the late Elizabeth, The Queen Mother, but which was originally built in the thirteenth century as a hunting lodge for the Scottish Crown, apparently walk the ghosts of the 'Grey Lady' and the 2nd Lord Glamis, Earl Beardie.

In Ireland, near Dublin, at Killakee House, built in 1765 as a hunting lodge for the Connolly family, there has supposedly been seen black cats, blue nuns and an Indian man, while in England, at a pub which stands on the site of Manor

Lodge, Sheffield (the sporting residence of various Earls of Shrewsbury mentioned in *How The Lodge Came About*), occasionally appears the apparition of a figure - thought by some to be a prisoner of state once housed at the Lodge. At The Dering Arms, Kent, is sometimes seen an old lady in a bonnet. This particular pub, situated in Pluckley - said to be the most haunted village in England - was originally another old hunting lodge but who the old lady was, or what the significance of her appearance is not really made clear in any records.

Another lady, this time wearing a red riding habit, is reputed to ride towards Gwrych Castle at Llanddulas in Wales, and is reckoned to be a previous owner killed in an accident on the hunting field: why she should be wearing red is open to speculation as it is not a colour that ladies would ever have worn whilst out following hounds. Also in Wales, at Denbigh Moors, there are the ruins of a hunting lodge called 'Plas Pren' - around which is said to have been observed a moving skeleton with glowing bones. Interestingly (whether it has its own ghost or not) also at Denbigh Moors is sited another, far more recent lodge, this time one built as a shooting lodge in the 1890s for the first Viscount Devonport (see also *Location, Location, Location*).

DUNDONNELL FOREST, Ross (32).

Area—30,000 acres of forest.

Bag—40 stags, besides 200 grouse, 130 rabbits, hares, pheasants, partridges, duck, etc.

Fishing—On 2 miles of the Dundonnell river there is fair salmon fishing, also salmon and sea trout fishing in the Gruinard river and Loch-na-Shallag. Brown trout is also fished on several lochs on the moor.

Accommodation of House—5 public rooms, 7 bedrooms, 2 dressing rooms, with extensive servants' accommodation. Coachhouses, 10-stalled stable, with accommodation for coachman and gillies.

Station—Garve (32 m.), Highland Railway.

Pier—Ullapool (6 m.)

P. & T. Office—Dundonnell (¼ m.)

Doctors—Ullapool (6 m.)

Churches—Ditto.

Supplies—Ditto.

General Remarks—In addition to the house at Dundonnell, there is a small lodge at Achnivie, with 1 sitting room and 4 bedrooms and keepers' accommodation. There is also a comfortable house at Gruinard with stables and coachhouse.

Owner—HUGH MACKENZIE.

Details of the lettings available at Dundonell Lodge in 1905

Dundonell Lodge, Ross-shire, circa 1870

LUNCHEON LODGES

✣

DURING THE LATE VICTORIAN PERIOD, some English and Welsh landowners with very large estates constructed luncheon lodges at various points of their property in order to enable guns shooting over a remote beat to lunch under cover – particularly if the main house was some distance away. The 1st Duke of Westminster, for example, built Eaton Lodge on his Eaton estate in Cheshire, so as to provide dining facilities for Guns shooting in Eaton Park. A commodious property, with accommodation for a gamekeeper and his wife (who also carried out caretaking duties as and when necessary), the lodge later became the retirement home of Anne, Duchess of Westminster, widow of the second duke.

Purpose-built Victorian luncheon lodges could also be found on the Duke of Portland's Welbeck Abbey estate in Nottinghamshire; at The Hendre, Lord Llangattock's estate in Monmouthshire (sadly now in ruins); and at Hursley in Hampshire (demolished long ago), where, according to local tradition, the Prince of Wales (later King Edward VII) is said to have played cards in between pheasant drives! On Brownsea Island in Dorset, a wooden Swiss style cottage standing on staddle stones (as at Hursley, now also demolished), known simply as the 'shooting lodge', was used as a dining room by late Victorian and Edwardian sportsman. At the latter, there was no such provision for the keepers, loaders and beaters though, all of whom sat outside eating chunks of homemade bread and Brownsea cheese…as well as quaffing copious amounts of ginger beer!

Generally, it was not unusual for a pre-prepared three course luncheon, fine wines or champagne and a supply of cigars to be transported by trap or pannier ponies from the kitchens at the 'big house' to a luncheon lodge on the morning of a shoot – together with crockery, cutlery, napery and silverware. After the lodge had been thoroughly cleaned and dusted by a couple of maids, fires would be lit, food heated on a small stove in an ante-room, and the dining table laid up in readiness for the arrival of the Guns. Lunch, itself, would be served by the butler, assisted by two or three footmen.

Dependant on status!

Shoot luncheons on the Belvoir estate in Leicestershire were served in great style during the first three decades of the twentieth century: they might have taken place in the castle itself, at 'Woodlands' (the head keeper's house), in a farmhouse, or in the luncheon lodge on the bottom carriage drive at Stathern – the actual venue being dependant upon the beat being shot over, or the social status of the guests. According to Burnell Grass, whose father, Fred Grass, was head keeper on the estate at the time, lunch in the lodge – a thatched wooden hut with a circular walnut dining table – was always a prestigious occasion. The ladies would drive down from the castle to join the Guns for lunch, which commenced promptly at one o'clock. The host, the Duke of Rutland, would personally serve the soup to his guests, after which the butler and liveried footmen would serve the main course, the sweet and victuals. Before the luncheon was completely over, the head keeper would enter the lodge and announce the details of the morning's bag to the guests, then have a brief chat with the Duke about the day's progress. This was a signal for the Guns to prepare to leave the lodge for the first drive of the afternoon.

Authors' Note: the luncheon lodge at Belvoir fell in to disuse decades ago and although the location of the actual site can still be seen, almost nothing is left of the building itself.

At the other end of the scale, a luncheon lodge lunch in the late Victorian period might simply be a D.I.Y. affair. According to Sir Algernon West, Chairman of the Inland Revenue Board from 1881 until 1892, it was the custom at some country houses for men going shooting 'to make themselves sandwiches from the cold meat which, with perhaps an egg, constituted the ordinary breakfast.' As a further example, grouse shooting guests of Squire Thomas Yorke, a major landowner in Upper Niddderdale, North Yorkshire, had to prepare their own ham sandwiches at the breakfast table and pack them in their pockets prior to starting for the grouse moor at 7.30 am, eating the sandwiches at lunch time in a stone-built hut on the moor, washed down with a nip from their flasks.

EDWARDIAN TIMES AND BEYOND

Later, from Edwardian times until after the Second World War, it was either 'feast or famine' – and mainly famine! Apparently, according to Jonathan Garnier Ruffer writing in *The Big Shots* (originally published by Debretts in 1977), lunch was never a sumptuous feast and at Holkham during the very first years of the twentieth century, '…was a pretty Spartan affair. Talking was discouraged, as it might upset the birds. One was allowed to sit down if one wanted, though it was not recommended, and the meal itself consisted of a few sandwiches hastily swallowed, and nothing to drink at all unless someone had the foresight to bring some brandy in a flask.'

In his memoirs, 'Porchey', 6th Earl of Carnarvon, recalled that, in the 1920s, most shooting parties, especially when on the grouse moors and partridge manors, were fortunate if they received sandwiches, a piece of cake, fruit, beer and, at the end of the day, a cold drink 'while the bag was being counted by the keepers'. In 1942, Jan Kosma, participating in a pheasant shoot for the first time, was surprised when lunchtime came round and food was taken in a barn. 'When we entered, their lordships, commodores and colonels tried to find seats on some dirty sacks and began to take food from their haversacks…'

Times were seemingly different after the Second World War – in 1951, sportsman and author, E C Keith suggested that 'there was a time when we all regarded the shooting lunch as a waste of time', but that with the passing of years, 'the amenities of the day interest as much as the actual killing. And in that state of mind a reasonably comfortable lunch is essential.' Furthermore, in his book *Shoots and Shooting* (Country Life Ltd), he was of the opinion that he would 'be horrified now if it was suggested that this should be replaced by a packet of sandwiches… Many "elderlies" like to appear Spartan and tough, but I doubt whether that adds anything to their enjoyment, or years…But times have changed. The beaters and guns are now conveyed in lorries or cars, so it is only a matter of minutes to transport the whole shooting company to any point which is most convenient for a well-ordered and satisfactory lunch.'

So it is, that, in the twenty-first century, almost every commercially-driven shoot retires to the shooting lodge or main house for lunch. There are, of course, still those 'die-hards' who partake of a sandwich in a cold, draughty barn – and say they enjoy their day just as equally but, for the majority, a luncheon hut or comfortable dining room is essential.

In his book *Pastoral Symphony*, published by Swan Hill Press in 1993, the author, journalist and one-time Fleet Street editor, Chapman Pincher, mentioned that whilst a sandwich lunch in a barn was thoroughly acceptable, 'the warm environment of a house or shooting lodge is very welcome to most guns, especially in bad weather, and makes for pleasurable relaxation and good fellowship. However, coupled with the "elevens" which many shoots serve, the extra intake of calories may more than replace the ounces of excess weight burned off by the activity. At Broadlands I experienced the ultimate in "elevens" when, after the first stand, one of the guests sent his driver-butler round with vintage champagne and a tray bearing hard-boiled eggs cut in half and a large tin of the best caviare!'

AS IT IS TODAY

Lunch venues range from the simple to the grand; from the traditional to the quirky – but common to them all is the camaraderie: without which no shooting day would be complete. The early morning gathering gives the opportunity for coffee – and the prospect of getting to know others who are going to share your day – and, if you know them already, a chance to catch up on life since you last met. A mid-morning break (or, as seen on many a shoot, a 'champagne stop' after the first drive!) can, with an imaginative host, include far more than the usual hot sausages or sausage rolls (kept warm in tin-foil and under tea-towels in the compulsory wicker basket) and 'bull-shot' or soup. Lunch is, though, for many, the day's focal point – be it sandwiches in a barn or a quite swish and lavish occasion.

The Grecian Temple, Chillington Hall

Designed to complement parkland laid out by Capability Brown, the Grecian Temple at Chillington Hall in Staffordshire was erected for Thomas Giffard during the late eighteenth century. The building is functional as well as being decorative, having the benefit of a two bed-roomed gamekeeper's house attached at the back. The Temple continued to serve as a keeper's residence until the mid-1960s when the final incumbent, Jim Parsons, left. Today, the Temple is used as a venue for shoot lunches by John Giffard, the current owner of Chillington.

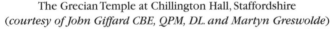

The Grecian Temple at Chillington Hall, Staffordshire
(*courtesy of John Giffard CBE, QPM, DL. and Martyn Greswolde*)

The Shooting Lodge, Yattendon Court

The Shooting Lodge at Yattendon Court, Berkshire (*courtesy of C G Hallam*)

Purpose-built in the early 1930s for the newspaper magnate, Edward Iliffe (1st Lord Iliffe), the shooting lodge at Yattendon Court near Newbury in Berkshire, is possibly one of the very first 'modern' luncheon lodges. It not only boasts a stylish dining room on the ground floor with oak fittings and furnishings together with cloakrooms, a kitchen and a loaders' room (which was used as a location set for the 1993 television series, *The Wartime Kitchen & Garden*), but also has a flat above to accommodate the estate's head gamekeeper and his family. The game larder is situated a short distance away from the lodge and combines game storage facilities with a beater's room complete with a fireplace around which they might gather on cold and wet days for a sandwich and a beer.

The Dining Room, Lees Court Shooting Lodge

The Shooting Lodge at Lees Court Estate in Kent provides guests with a range of facilities in a converted eighteenth century barn and not only boasts a luxurious dining room and a comfortable sitting room but also has a large indoor swimming pool. The Countess Sondes, the host, who is passionate about game shooting, has created a unique atmosphere where everyone is treated as a personal guest rather than as a paying Gun.

The Lime Caves, Lees Court

Originally excavated to enable lime to be extracted from subterranean deposits for agricultural purposes, these man-made caves now serve as an 'elevenses' point on the Lees Court shoot. Guns are offered tea, coffee or something a little stronger, together with home-made honey-glazed sausages or other snack items, all served by the butler and his staff.

A formal dining table for lunch at Lees Court shooting lodge…
(*courtesy of the Countess Sondes*)

…and wonderful rural surroundings for elevenses (*courtesy of C G Hallam*)

Dell, Inverness-shire

Whilst there is much more pertaining to Dell elsewhere in this book, as far as the subject of food is concerned, owner Jeremy Finnis tells us that:'Shooting parties at Dell take their elevenses in the log cabin on Loch Kemp, where the views are stunning.'The shoot supper is, though,'quite formal and taken in the dining room'.

The Dell dining room set out for an evening meal…

…and Guns have a wonderful view of Loch Kemp as they take their elevenses near or in the log cabin

The Towers, Llanarmon

Bobby McAlpine's superb shoot is about thirty-five miles from Chester and sits in the Ceiriog valley with views of the fabulous Berwyn Hills. Considered by many to provide the best of shooting in Wales, there are, though, those for whom the high-point of the day is lunch at The Towers!

Mr McAlpine mentions that 'The Towers was a substantial house of three storeys although my grandfather never put his guests up there. My father reduced the house substantially to one storey in the 1960s, when he enlarged the dining room and built on toilet facilities, though because he owned the Hand hotel, he did not put in a kitchen, I added this when I inherited the shoot.'

The Towers before alteration in the 1960s... (*courtesy of Bobby McAlpine*)

He goes on to say, 'the house has an interesting history in that it was built sometime in the mid 1800s but there is no exact record of the year. We do know that the only two years it was used as a private residence were 1900 and 1901, when Colonel West (the West Arms, in the village was named after him) lived there. The Cornwallis West's were the in-laws of "Bendor", the 2nd Duke of Westminster. He at some point acquired Llanarmon from his father in-law and it was because after the break-up of his first marriage that he so disliked his mother in-law that he decided to rid himself of the family associations. My grandfather, Sir Alfred McAlpine, was in the right place at the right time and rented the shoot in 1923 and bought the estate in 1931.'

… and as it is today (*courtesy of Bobby McAlpine and Charlie Caminada*)

Pull up the drawbridge!

A small shoot in the Midlands takes its lunch breaks in a converted barn – which is accessed via a covered 'drawbridge' over a pond. Once inside, beaters and Guns can rest in very comfortable surroundings indeed...which, on a wet day, must make returning outdoors for the afternoon's sport, quite a daunting prospect!

Guns and beaters enter this luncheon barn via a covered drawbridge...

...and once inside, have very comfortable surroundings (*both photos courtesy of Rupert Stephenson*)

The Shoot Luncheon Barn, Squirrel's Hall

Situated in the heart of 'Constable Country' in the beautiful Dedham Vale on the Essex-Suffolk border, the 800 acre Squirrel's Hall shoot has been managed by sporting tenant and head gamekeeper, Dean Harris, and his wife, Jo, (one of less than 100 full-time lady gamekeepers in Great Britain) for the past twelve years. The luncheon barn, itself, which dates back to the sixteenth century, provides simple yet homely accommodation for the superlative home-made shoot lunches produced by Dean's in-house cook, Lisa Pugh, who uses locally sourced ingredients whenever possible.

Interior of the luncheon barn at Squirrel's Hall...

Lunchtime chat at Squirrel's Hall
(*both photos courtesy of Dean and Jo Harris*)

'The Lounge', The Shoot Barn, Manor Farm, Teffont Magna

As mentioned earlier, Edward Waddington's 2,600 acre Teffont Magna shoot is considered by many to be one of 'Wiltshire's best kept secrets'. Situated amidst rolling downland fifteen miles west of Salisbury, it provides some magnificently testing birds and, as an added bonus, morning coffee, luncheon and afternoon tea are all served in a wonderful old converted barn adjacent to the host's house. The star attraction of the barn, apart from the magnificent traditional country house style dining room, is the shoot lounge which is reminiscent of an Edwardian smoking room, complete with comfortable sofas, sporting paintings, stuffed 'trophies of the chase' and an assortment of quirky antiques!

Comfort and sustenance of the best kind can be found on Ed Waddington's shoot at Teffont Magna (*courtesy of C G Hallam*)

A New Forest sojourn

At the Lyburn shoot, deep in the heart of the New Forest, lunch is taken under the cover of an open-fronted corrugated-clad building. Whilst some might look on anxiously and apprehensively, the men do what, traditionally, men do best and, even if they go nowhere a cooking implement for the remainder of the year, produce a very impressive barbeque for everyone involved in the day!

Alfresco dining in the New Forest (*courtesy of Tony Moss*)

Before leaving the subject of shooting luncheon lodges and dining places, we thought it well worthwhile mentioning a type of building that very definitely combines rustic charm and new technology! Already well-known for their range of reproduction shepherds' huts, Richard Lee and his team at Plankbridge Hutmakers, Piddlehinton in rural Dorset, have begun manufacturing shepherds' huts with the specific needs of sportsmen in mind.

Produced to a traditional design, but benefiting from insulation, solar power and other modern features, these mobile huts can be adapted to provide overnight accommodation for fishermen or river keepers and have recently built their first shoot luncheon hut for a Dorset estate.

Plankbridge featured greatly in the national media in 2012 when their 'Shepherds' Hut Garden' was awarded a Silver Medal at the RHS Chelsea Flower Show. Their huts also serve as an unusual guest bedroom, study, playroom, and have a variety of other applications.

A novel shoot luncheon hut designed and built by Plankbridge Hutmakers (*courtesy of Plankbridge Hutmakers, Dorset*)

FISHING HUTS

Fishing huts, inevitably, come in all shapes and sizes, ranging from the pretty 'chocolate box' style wooden huts with thatched roofs, commonly found alongside south country trout streams and rivers, to the functional stone built bothies associated with many of the great Scottish salmon waters. In addition, a variety of other buildings or vehicles have, in recent decades, been pressed into service as improvised, yet permanent fishing huts on rivers throughout Great Britain. These include historic or reproduction wheeled shepherds' huts, caravans, pre-fabricated garden sheds, a Nissen air raid shelter of World War Two vintage (in use on the river Test in Hampshire), and a former bus, which doubles as both a fishing hut and river watcher's residence near the mouth of the Barvas river on the Isle of Lewis in the Outer Hebrides.

Bossington, Hampshire

Considered by many to be the first home of chalk-stream fly-fishing, the whole of the River Test is picturesque and, for the fishing purist, 'its gin-clear water and abundance of weed make it ideal for wild and stocked brown trout…' Along its length can be seen numerous thatched shelters, but we would argue that not many can be more delightful than the Victorian fishing hut at Bossington! It might, however, not still be in existence were it not for the fact that Sir Richard Fairey (founder of the Fairey Aviation Company), bought the Bossington Estate in 1937 and, being a keen and expert fisherman, maintained and improved the water meadows, river and its tributaries – and, of course, the existing fishing huts. The Bossington Estate is now owned by his granddaughter, Sarah Jane Fairey, and continues to attract fishermen from all over the world…as can be seen in this quote from an article, 'England's Top Fly Fishing Rivers' which was published in America's *Forbes Life Magazine*:

BETWEEN 11:30 and 1:00 on our day of fishing…Bossington…, Peter and I caught and released three trout apiece – vividly colored, hard-fighting browns ranging from one and a half to four pounds. We took our lunch of Brie-and-salmon sandwiches and prosciutto-wrapped pears inside the beat's comfortable new fishing hut, where old rods were suspended from the ceiling and fishing prints hung on the walls. Late that afternoon we walked up to a large, slow pool above a weir and had a couple more hours of peerless dry-fly-fishing.

It is on the Home Beat, though, where the Victorian hut stands – a perfect place for a long, leisurely lunch: as a fisherman of great experience once recently 'tweeted' for all to see, 'lunching…in style…[in] perhaps the best fishing hut in the world.'

This delightful Victorian fishing hut can be found on the Home Beat at Bossington…

…the interior is no less charming, especially when set out ready for lunch!
(both photos courtesy of Howard Taylor/www.upstreamdryfly.com)

The famous school Winchester College is somewhat unusual in that, although it owns the piscatorial rights on five miles of the Itchen (divided into nine beats), it only has one small fishing hut which was built 'off the shelf' in the 1990s. Bursar Robin Chute says that a fishing club was 'was formed in 1910 although Isaac Walton fished our water and all the great Old Wykehamist fishermen like Grey and Skues fished here as boys. We have only one small car park and inadequate hut – although it is perfectly adequate for the boys.'

The fishing lodge at East Lodge, Twyford, Hampshire (*courtesy of Dick Bronks*)

Elsewhere along the Itchen, fishing huts are both pleasing to the eye and useful: at East Lodge, Twyford, for example, fishing guests get the very best of both worlds – great chalk stream fishing and a well appointed main lodge on the bank in which rest or have lunch. Attached is a rod-room.

Functional rather than formal

As has already been mentioned above, any trip along the River Test will discover a plentiful supply of particularly attractive, yet simple fishing huts used on a daily basis by trout fishermen who wish to eat their packets of sandwiches, shelter from the rain or tie a few flies 'on the go'.

Generally, lunch, in angling terms, is, of course, often a solitary affair with a Rod dining alone in a fishing hut, on the river bank, in a boat or, in some cases, in the company of his or her ghillie. Eaten primarily to fortify the 'inner man' the food tends to be much less sophisticated than that found at a shoot lunch and can be often be chosen from a menu of comestibles, which are packed in a hamper by kitchen staff at a sporting lodge or hotel. Alternatively, it might simply consist of D.I.Y. sandwiches made at the breakfast table (even titled angling guests of Viscount Leverhulme at Lews Castle were expected to make their own sandwiches at the breakfast table during the early 1920s).

If the 'fish are on', an angler is far more likely to concentrate on catching trout or salmon and eat his lunch on an 'as and when' basis rather than make a feast of it!

Lunch in the Outer Hebrides

Guests staying at a well known salmon fishery in the Outer Hebrides can choose from a selection of luncheon items which are put out by the lodge staff every morning. These include good quality sandwiches with various fillings, made from either brown or white bread, with pickle, horseradish and other optional extras; fruit cake; pork pies and other savouries. Beverages on offer range from tea, coffee and water to soup, wine and beer. The packed lunch is then put into a fishing bag by staff – along with napkins, cutlery, crockery and condiments – and given to the rod's ghillie to carry prior to departure for the river or lochs. (If the lunch is to be eaten in a fishing hut, the ghillie is also responsible for ensuring that the hut is clean prior to use!)

Lunch at Charles Cotton's Fishing House

Situated near Hartington, on the county borders of Staffordshire and Derbyshire, Charles Cotton, a friend of Izaak Walton, had his unique fishing house built in 1674 on 'a kind of peninsula, with a delicate clear river about it.' Used as a refuge whilst fishing, it also proved invaluable as a luncheon hut when hot food was brought down from nearby Beresford Hall.

The fireplace at Charles Cotton's stone fishing house is a place for contemplation…

Although, lunch today is perhaps more likely to be a cold collation, the venue is just as it always was, full of charm and atmosphere. As Michael Collins, the present owner of the fishing house says; 'I imagine there's many a fisherman's tale that has been told beside this fire!'

...and conversation (*both photos courtesy of Graham Downing*)

An interesting French fishing hut

Near Airvault, France, at the corner of what was once a totally walled estate, stands an interesting and attractive building which was once used as a shelter for fishermen on the river that passes close-by. The best way of describing it would be to use the French name 'borie' – used to denote any of the many small buildings that can be found throughout France, but which are perhaps most

A French 'borie' – used as a shelter and lunchtime eating place for fishermen

commonly seen in the south-east regions. Technically, however, such buildings (which have been used for both animal and human shelter for literally hundreds of years), should be constructed in dry-stone rather than lime-cemented as this one is.

Costing nothing to build – only the labourer's time – 'bories' were a good way of using up the plentiful supply of stones that emerged as ground was ploughed and cultivated. The fact that stones were put to good use rather than merely stacked up randomly will, no doubt, have been much appreciated by anglers and other sportsmen over the generations when caught out by an unexpected heavy shower!

LUNCH ON THE HUNTING FIELD

Out hunting, there has never been any such thing as a luncheon lodge of any kind! Times have changed since the Hunting Act of 2004 and so, with 'trail-hunting' and 'drag-hunting', there is every opportunity between 'draws' to partake of a little organised sustenance. In the past, however, despite there being a considerable number of places built as overnight or seasonal accommodation for dyed-in-the wool followers of hounds, there were absolutely no temporary lodges set aside as 'refuelling' points during a day's hunting. There was a simple reason for this and it is that packs of hounds in full flight do not generally stop for lunch! After a decent breakfast and possibly a sausage roll or similar at the meet, the best one could have done would have been to pack a sandwich in the pocket of your hunting jacket and eat it during a quiet moment.

No matter where they meet, hound packs rarely, if ever, have any
particular lodge location set-aside for lunch
(*courtesy of Jeremy Whaley/South Downs Bloodhounds*)

A Pennine tradition

There is, though, one area of the British Isles where you might find rare exceptions to this rule, and that is in the 'mill' valleys of West Yorkshire. Unlike most packs of hounds who traditionally meet at 11.00am, the Colne Valley, the Holme Valley and their ilk have, on a Saturday, usually met at 10.30am, stopped for lunch a couple of hours or so later and then, at 1.30 or 2.00 in the afternoon, begun again (sometimes even from a different location). At their mid-week meets, there is, generally, just a single afternoon turnout.

The reason behind this unique Pennine tradition is thought to be that this split hunting was originally created in order that, whilst the gentry who didn't have to toil to make a living, could enjoy their sport all day, the local mill workers (always an enthusiastic bunch of men when it came to following hounds in days gone by) could join the hunt after their morning shift. Whatever the original reason, the gap between morning and afternoon hunting is, more often than not, spent in a local pub (the venue for a good many of the meets) and, as well as the opportunity for a pint (or two) of Yorkshire beer, there will often be available, sandwiches, hot-pot or a steaming bowl of pie and peas!

The Long Drop
Leigh Manor Shoot Lodge, Shropshire
(courtesy David Stacey)

BIBLIOGRAPHY, FURTHER READING, REFERENCES AND SOURCES

Alexander, Karen (Ed): *The Changing Year*; The Field/Harmsworth Active, 1993

Arris, Roy: *The Atlantic Salmon Atlas*; Silver Run Publishing, 2003

Author unknown, but variously given as 'A Member of the Aristocracy' or, 'By the author of 'Manners and Tone of Good Society': *The Servants' Practical Guide - a handbook of duties and rules*; F Warne & Co, 1880

Beaufort, Duke of: *Fox-Hunting*; David & Charles, 1980

Beaufort, 8th Duke; Morris, Mowbray: *Hunting* (part of the 'Badminton' series); Longmans, Green and Co., New Edition 1906

Billett, Michael: *A History of English Country Sports*; Robert Hale Ltd, 1994

Bradshaw, George: *Bradshaw's Handbook*; originally published in 1863. Old House, 2012

Braithwaite, Cecil: *Happy Days with Rod, Gun and Bat*; published privately, no date but probably late 1940s

Braithwaite, Geoffrey: *Fine Feathers and Fish*; published privately 1971

Brooks, Howard; White, Andrew; Nicholls, Francis: *The Lost Tudor Hunting Lodge at Wormingford*; Colchester Archaeological Group, 2010

Carlton, H.W: *Spaniels: Their Breaking for Sport and Field Trials*; The Field Press Ltd, 1915

Carnarvon, Earl of: *Ermine Tales*; Weidenfeld and Nicolson, 1980

Craigie, Eric: *Irish Sporting Sketches*; The Lilliput Press, 1984

Denys, Bt., Sir Francis: *Sporting Journal*; unpublished manuscript

Dusi, Isabella: *Vanilla Beans & Brodo - real life in the hills of Tuscany*; Simon & Schuster UK Ltd, 2001

Field, The: *Where to Fish*, 1925–1940

Ford, Cyril; Woodcock, C B: *Hunting in The Holme Valley - an illustrated history of the working man's hunt*; published privately, 1986

Foster, Muriel: *Muriel Foster's Fishing Diary*; Michael Joseph, 1980

Fouin, François Louis Pierre: *Glen Tanar - valley of echoes and hidden treasures*; Leopard Press, 2010

Gathorne-Hardy, Alfred E: *My Happy Hunting Grounds*; Longmans, Green & Co., 1914

Godwin, Rev. G N: *The Green Lanes of Hampshire, Surrey and Sussex*; c.1880

Harvey, Tony: *If St Peter Has Hounds*; Paul Rackham Ltd, 1998

Hastings, Macdonald: *Macdonald Hastings' Country Book - a personal anthology*; George Newnes Ltd, 1961

Hely-Hutchinson, Rev. George: *Twenty Years*

Reminiscences of The Lews; Bickers & Son, 1871

Hobson, J C Jeremy: *The Shoot Lunch*; Quiller, 2011

Holt, Peter: *The Keen Foxhunter's Miscellany*; Quiller, 2010

Hutchinson, Margaret M; Holland, Penny (Ed): *An Edwardian Childhood - the making of a naturalist*; 4th New Edition, John Owen Smith, 2003

Inverness Courier, The: various articles between 1817–1936

Jefferies, Richard: *The Gamekeeper at Home* 1878 (and countless reprints since)

Jones, David S D: *Amhuinnsuidhe and North Harris - the history of an Outer Hebridean Sporting Estate*; published privately, 2011

Jones, David S D: *Gamekeeping Tales from the Grass Family*; published privately, 2012

Jones, David S D: *The Eishken Estate - a history*; Comunn Eachdraidh na Pairc, 2009

Jones, David S D: *The Sporting Estates of the Outer Hebrides - past and present*; published privately, 2008

Keith, E.C.: *Shoots and Shooting*, Country Life Ltd, 1951

Kite, Oliver: *A Fisherman's Diary*; Andre Deutch, 1969

Lambton, Lucinda: *Palaces for Pigs - animal architecture and other beastly buildings*; English Heritage, 2011

Lewis, Joan: *The Cotswold Cook Book*; Global Publications, 1990

Leyden, John: *Journal of a Tour in The Highlands and Western Islands of Scotland*; 1800

Mackay, John: *Memories of Grimersta*; un-published manuscript

Maciver, Evander: *Memoirs of a Highland Gentleman*; published privately, 1905

Malcolm, George; Maxwell, Aymer: *Grouse and Grouse Moors*; Adam & Charles Black, 1910

Maclean, Norman: *A River Runs Through It*; University of Chicago Press, 1976

Marren, Peter: *The Wild Woods - a regional guide to Britain's ancient woodland*; David & Charles, 1992

Marriat-Ferguson, J E: *Visiting Home*; published privately, 1905

Mason, Jill: *'Away; My Lads, Away'*; published privately, 2011

Miller, Christian: *A Childhood in Scotland*; John Murray, 1979

Mursell, Norman: *Come Dawn, Come Dusk - fifty years a gamekeeper*; George Allen & Unwin, 1981

Musson, Jeremy: *Up and Down Stairs - the history of the country house servant*; James Murray, 2009

Orchard-Lisle, Jo: *Fishing Huts - the angler's sanctuary*; Excellent Press, 2008

Palmer, Arnold: *Movable Feasts - fluctuations in mealtimes*; originally published by Oxford University Press in 1952 - and re-printed by Oxford Paperbacks, 1984

Pern, Andrew: *Black Pudding & Foie Gras*; Face, 2008

Pincher, Chapman: *Pastoral Symphony - a bumpkin's tribute to country joys*; Swan Hill Press, 1993

Poole, R.W. F: *Hunting - an introductory handbook*; David & Charles, 1988

Porter, Val: *Milland: The Book*; Milland Memories Group, 2003

Richardson, Charles: *The Complete Foxhunter*; Methuen, 1908

Ruffer, JG: *The Big Shots - Edwardian Shooting Parties*; first published by Debretts, 1977. New edition of 2nd revised edition, Quiller 2003

Sassoon, Siegfried: *Memoirs of a Fox-hunting Man*; Faber and Faber 1928

'Scrutator': *Recollections of a Foxhunter*; Hurst & Blackett, 1861

Siyabona Africa Travel Ltd: *Africa Lodge Accommodation and Safari Guide*; 2012

The David S D Jones Gamekeeping Archive

The David S D Jones Western Isles Countrysports Archive and Photographic Collection

Vandervell, Anthony; Coles, Charles: *Game and the English Landscape - the influence of the chase on sporting art and scenery*; Debrett's Peerage Ltd, 1980

Williamson, Tom: *The Archaeology of Rabbit Warrens* (Shire Books 2006)

INDEX

INDEX